FAMILIES LEARNING TOGETHER

The Home and School Institute

A Wallaby Book
Published by Simon & Schuster
New York

Copyright © 1980 by The Home and School Institute
All rights reserved
No part of this publication may be reproduced, stored in a retrieval system, or transmitted in any form or by any means, electronic, mechanical, photocopy, recording, or otherwise, without prior written permission from the Home and School Institute, c/o Trinity College, Washington, D.C. 20017.

Published by Wallaby Books, A Simon & Schuster Division of Gulf & Western Corporation, Simon & Schuster Building, 1230 Avenue of the Americas, New York, New York 10020

WALLABY and colophon are trademarks of Simon & Schuster

First Wallaby Books Printing September 1981
10 9 8 7 6 5 4 3 2 1
Manufactured in the United States of America

Library of Congress Cataloging in Publication Data
Main entry under title:

Families learning together.

 "A Wallaby book."
 Previous ed.: Washington, D.C.: Home and School Institute, 1980.
 1. Parenting—United States. 2. Life skills—United States. 3. Domestic education—United States. I. Home and School Institute (Washington, D.C.)
HQ755.8.F35   1981   649′.68   81-10308 AACR2
ISBN 0-671-43576-0

Welcome to Families Learning Together

This is a program of easy activities to help you and all your family learn useful skills together.

This program is made up of 48 activities for the home that are fun and also help your children achieve more in school. We call these activities "recipes for learning." They use the supermarket, the kitchen and the neighborhood.

These activities don't cost money. You can do them together with your children, even on a busy day. They are a new kind of homework. They do not duplicate what children do in school. They use everyday objects (things you have in your home). They give your child practice in basic reading and math skills and in attitudes and behaviors needed for success.

In this handbook you will find 24 reading and 24 math activities. They were designed for families with children in kindergarten to grade six.

These activities also provide practical tips for adults in daily life skills and for parents in such areas as how to shop wisely, how to provide safety in the home, and how to be a more effective parent.

Research has shown that families—your family and your home—are very important to children's achievement. These "recipe" activities have been developed to help you help your children.

Thousands of families across the nation have tested these activities. They are enthusiastic. They find that doing activities together make everyday moments more exciting and rewarding. Family members learn more about each other and more about themselves. Everyone in and near the family is involved—grandparents, teenagers, friends, neighbors.

In doing these activities, choose the ones you want to do. Pick those that appeal to your family. Anyone can assist children in doing the activities. Don't worry about doing anything wrong in this home teaching. You can't do it wrong and neither can your child. Be imaginative. Use your own ideas to make the activities even more enjoyable for your family.

For more details on this program, see the "Introduction" for the program's background and the section entitled "The Return of the Teaching Parent."

We are pleased to share this special adventure in family learning with you.

The HSI Philosophy Brings Together Current Research and Old-Fashioned Common Sense

The philosophy underlying **Families Learning Together** is built directly on both the needs and the potential of all children and of their families.

Children need to and can learn attitudes and skills that will help them achieve in school and out.

Parents and other adults need to and can achieve greater competence in helping children develop as people and in building children's abilities for academic achievement.

These are the most important tasks in our society.

Families Learning Together was developed to address these tasks by translating them into manageable and "do-able" actions. This program is designed to prevent families from feeling helpless and to ensure individual family competencies. These activities have been tested and have been shown to work effectively and easily.

Bringing families together is a real challenge today when children and parents are no longer tied to the home in the same way as they were in earlier times. With a growing number of two parent working families, the appeal of television and the outside world, stresses on the family often serve to pull parent and child apart.

The strength of this program is that it brings parent and child back together in their homes and in their communities.

The program offers an integrated approach to education which addresses children's needs for discipline, motivation and good work habits through activities with parents at home—activities that are needed and real in that they encompass daily life routines.

This is a new curriculum combining three basic ingredients:
- Children's reading and math skills in grades K–6.
- Adult basic knowledge in such daily life subjects as nutrition and consumerism.
- Tips to help adults be better parents.

This curriculum does not duplicate the work of the school. Children are in school only half of the days of the year. Direct, daily instructional time in the classroom by a teacher on a one-to-one basis, can be counted in minutes. Schools work with children in groups. Individual time and attention for each child in school is a goal. But, it is a reality in every home!

Families Learning Together is based on the premise that not even the best school can do the job alone. The home is the continuing, vital, coordinating center of children's education. Research supports this premise.

Research of the last two decades has shown that efforts of the schools which do not involve families do not result in achievement for children. These findings have strong implications for school policies and practices. The Home and School Institute (HSI), since 1964, has been working with school personnel and families to develop the educational partnership needed between the school and home. The Institute's experience and research indicate that priority attention should be given by schools to develop ways to involve families directly in the education of their own children.

There are several central reasons for this type of parent involvement. This approach:

(1) Has been linked to improved academic achievement by a continuing line of research. (A bibliography of this research is available from HSI.)

(2) Shares responsibility for education with the family—providing adults with basic strategies and guidance for use at home and in the community.

(3) Offers the greatest opportunity for widespread family involvement and sustained participation, appealing to the most basic parental motivation—the desire to help one's child do better.

(4) Provides for adults in their parenting role greater satisfaction and insights about their children. Mothers at home gain a sense of the importance of their maternal role. Mothers at work outside of the home are shown ways to combine the worlds of work and home.

The research supporting the home-teaching role is good news for working parents and single parents—for all adults coping with today's limited budget of resources and time. What this means is that families working together in convenient bits of time during their daily lives at home can build children's abilities painlessly and joyfully.

This is a self-help approach that is easy for teachers and parents to start and then continue—on their own. This method has been used successfully with all children—rural, urban, rich, poor, bilingual and handicapped.

Research, common sense and our nation's needs support this approach. Fulfilling a child's potential is a family's achievement, a community's strength, and a nation's security.

ACKNOWLEDGMENTS

The Home and School Institute wishes to recognize those who trust the basic strengths of all families and who have given generously of themselves and of their time to help all families help their children.

To the team of HSI staff members who worked together to prepare this publication. All are parents and all are professionals in education with long experience and strong commitment to real and meaningful family involvement in children's education:

**SANDRA PARKER COATES
NANCY G. HARTER
BEVERLY MATTOX
ANNE MYCHALUS
JAMES VAN DIEN, Ed.D.
JUNE WAREHAM**

To the thousands of families across the nation whose use of and acclaim for the first printing of the **Families Learning Together** program and whose contributions to the work of the Institute have made this second edition possible.

To the Board and the National Advisory Council of the Institute for their nurturing support and encouragement:

Miriam Bazelon, John Bottum, Misbah Khan, M.D., Marjorie Craig Benton, Ronald S. Brandt, Don Cameron, Elizabeth P. Campbell, Wilton S. Dillon, Jeremiah Floyd, Paul L. Houts, A. Sidney Johnson III, Tom C. Korologos, Leanna Landsmann, Nancy Larrick, Ann Y. Riley, Mitchell Rogovin, Carol F. Sulzberger, William L. Taylor, Carol H. Tice, Steven J. Wolin, M.D., Mildred Kiefer Wurf.

To the Charles Stewart Mott Foundation whose grant supported the initial development and field-testing of the program.

To The Council of the Great City Schools for recognizing the importance of the home-school partnership.

To the Publishing Group of Rockville, Maryland, and especially to Scott MacDonald for his creativity and assistance in the design of the **Families Learning Together** publication.

To Susan Lord, HSI Executive Secretary, for her unfailing help and special talents in ensuring that HSI serves as many families and schools across the nation as is possible.

To my own family for their understanding, for their wonderful ideas, and for their caring all through the years—past and present—as HSI pioneered to develop the framework of research and programming on which **Families Learning Together** is based.

Dorothy Rich, Ed.D., Founder and President
The Home and School Institute, Inc.

Photo credits for montage:

U.S. Department of Education:
American Education,
Department of the Navy:
Office of Information

TABLE OF CONTENTS

    Welcome to Families Learning Together 3

    The Families Learning Together Philosophy 4

    Acknowledgments 6

I.   **INTRODUCING THE PROGRAM** 9

    Simple And Effective 10

    How This Program Can Help You,
Your Family And Your Community 10

    The Return of the Teaching Parent 11

    Tips For Good Results 12

II.   **INTRODUCING THE "RECIPES"** 14

        Blueprint For Family Learning 16

    Reading: Grades Kindergarten To Third 18

        The Importance Of Me 20

        The Working World 22

        My Special Garden 24

        A Walk Through The Pages 26

        Everything Fits 28

        Let The Sun Shine 30

        Bottom Shelf Shopper 32

        The Best Greetings Are Free 34

        Health Care Messages 36

        Planning Ahead 38

        Water Tour 40

        TV: Choice Or Habit 42

    Mathematics: Grades Kindergarten To Third 44

        Sign Signals 46

        Numbers Galore 48

        Math On The Move 50

        Paper Bag Walk 52

        The Time Of Our Lives 54

        Food And Money 56

        Stepping Out 58

Water Magic		60
Weigh Me		62
Entertainments Near And Far		64
My Very Own Place		66
SOS		68
Reading: Grades Four To Six		70
Objects Tell Occupations		72
Visiting Older People		74
Business Walk		76
Family Directory		78
How Much Is It?		80
Fill In The Blanks		82
Personal Health File		84
Button, Button		86
What Do You Think?		88
Operation Alert		90
Child Care By The Hour		92
Who's In The News?		94
Mathematics: Grades Four To Six		96
About Town		98
Men, Women and Jobs		100
My Private Time Line		102
Energy Wise		104
It's My Turn		106
Making Money Count		108
Saving And Banking		110
Prices Going Up		112
The Best Buys Have It		114
Fractions For Friends		116
Weather Watch		118
What's In Your Food?		120

III. **SUCCESS IN SCHOOL STARTS AND CONTINUES AT HOME** 123

    From One Parent to Another 124

    About The Home and School Institute 126

I. INTRODUCING THE FAMILIES LEARNING TOGETHER PROGRAM

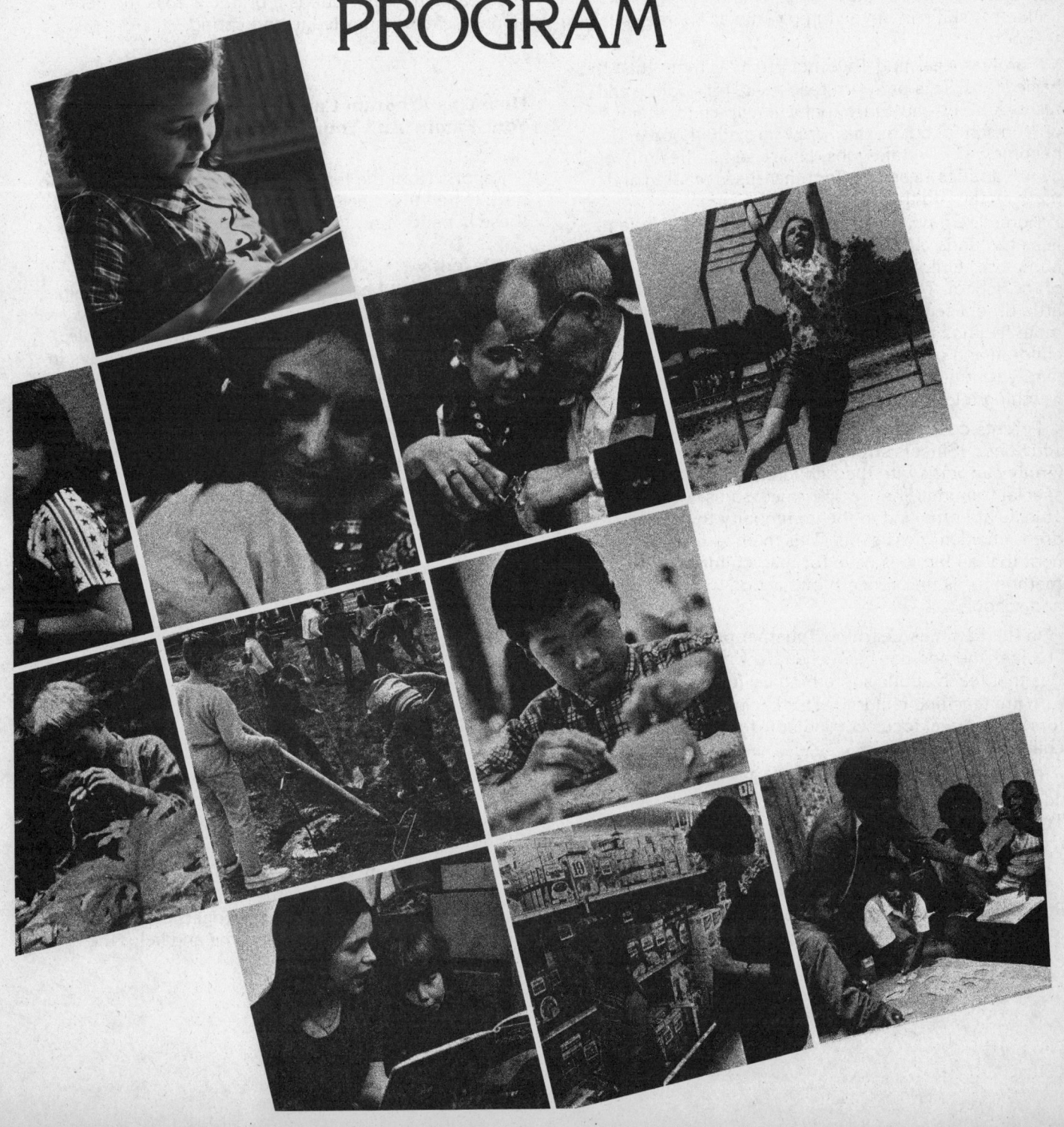

IT SEEMS SO SIMPLE: CAN THIS PROGRAM REALLY BE EFFECTIVE?

What Is It?

Background: **Families Learning Together** uses the Home and School Institute (HSI) educational method called home learning "recipes." These "recipes" center around activities that happen in daily life at home and in the neighborhood. This method builds children's skills by involving parents as "home-style" teachers.

Families Learning Together provides more than the basic skills. This program teaches self discipline and responsibility—attitudes that will help children not only in school but as they grow into adulthood and become citizens, take jobs, and raise families of their own. **Families Learning Together** fuses reading and math skills with the basic skills for living.

Home learning "recipes" are designed to give families new kinds of teaching tools. These activities for home use reinforce—they do not duplicate—the work of the school. The best "recipes" are those that take little time, use resources already on hand, and promote feelings of accomplishment and togetherness for children and parents. These activities fit into the daily family routine, at meals, at homework time or while watching television.

Parents do not need a teaching degree to do these activities. HSI feels strongly that any parent and any family can work with their children, without receiving special training. The "recipe" method uses ordinary objects at home and in the community to teach children school success skills. This method uses the concern that all families have for their children. This method turns this concern into action to help children and schools.

In the **Families Learning Together** program the "recipe" method has been changed to provide activities that teach adults something useful while they in turn are teaching children. This becomes what educators call a "dual-focus curriculum" for adults and for children.

Experts in the field say that this is the first time adult/child materials like this have been developed. The children's skill areas are reading and mathematics. The adult knowledge areas are: Health/Safety, Citizenship/Government and Law, Consumer Economics, Occupational Knowledge and Community Resources. The adult learning areas are the Adult Performance Level (APL) knowledge areas identified by the U.S. Department of Education.

The basic theme throughout is parenting and family life. Helping people to get along with each other and to solve problems is a skill found in all the "recipes." The parent and child topics in each "recipe" match each other: When children read to older people, parents learn about the needs of senior citizens today. When children learn to handle home emergencies, parents learn about community emergency telephone services.

This program is based on the belief that the family that learns together builds a bridge across the generations of shared knowledge and caring.

How This Program Can Help You, Your Family And Your Community

Reports from the families and from the teachers who have tested these activities show that you can expect these benefits from the use of this program:

As Parents

The **Families Learning Together** program will help you become more aware of your importance as a teacher to your children. The program will enable you to get involved in positive and practical ways in your children's education.

For Adult Learners

As adults, we often need motivation to continue our own learning beyond the classroom. There is no better motivation than helping our own children. All of these activities include daily life facts and parenting information.

For Your Children

Throughout **Families Learning Together,** you are encouraged to use your imagination and creativity. Children are born with the urge to grow and to learn. This book is all about helping children **realize** their potential and use their special gifts.

For Teachers

Teachers need the support and involvement of the home to ensure that children learn what gets taught in school. This program provides teachers with new ways to reinforce what's happening in school.

For The Community

Working and sharing together is what a community is all about. **Families Learning Together** is a self-help program that begins at home and helps the whole community.

THE RETURN OF THE TEACHING PARENT

The wise parent realizes that education begins and continues at home, even after children go to school.

Until recently some of the child care education experts who appear in print and on TV talk shows, warned parents not to teach children, not to expect too much, especially not to push. They said, in effect, "Take your hands off those children, relax, don't teach, let the school do it."

But, because of recent educational research and disappointments resulting from over-dependence on the school, we're learning about the importance of the home and of the neighborhood as vital places for learning.

All of this is not really new. Actually, it's old-fashioned in the best sense. Years ago parents taught their children at home. In the ranks of teaching parents are Rose Kennedy, Ida Eisenhower, and the mothers of Pablo Casals, Frank Lloyd Wright, and Booker T. Washington. They saw themselves as teachers of their own children. They believed in the achievement of their children.

These examples are extreme, but they make a valuable point. Before Frank Lloyd Wright was born, his mother decided he was to be an architect. She framed ten large wood engravings of Old English cathedrals and hung them in the nursery. Sister Elizabeth Kenny, famous for her work in treating infantile paralysis, had no other teacher than her mother who taught her the three R's in the evening at home. The list of achieving children of "pushy" parents goes on and on.

Adults today are better educated than ever before. The home is in a stronger position than ever before to help children develop and achieve. The home can be and must be the educational partner to the school. This is what **Families Learning Together** is all about.

Families across the nation using these "recipes" reported on their experiences. They said that they became aware of qualities in each other that they had not previously noticed, and they gained new insights about themselves. Here are some of their comments:

Parents
"I think this project has helped me in having my child think as well as make decisions."

"Becky is enjoying these activities. It is helping her learn. It is also something I can share and do with her."

"The whole family has enjoyed these activities. I think they have helped me in a way, more than they have helped my child in that I am developing more patience."

"My child is willing to assume more responsibility."

Children
"I feel better about doing school work now."

"I like school more now than before."

"I spend more time with my parents now."

Teachers
The teachers felt that by using this program the families became more aware of their roles as parents. Here are some of their comments:

"Parents and children seem to enjoy each other more."

"Parents are spending more time listening to children and helping them."

"Students are showing more enthusiasm and bringing in homework more often."

"They seem to like school better and show an improved self-image through feelings of accomplishment."

NOTE: Readers interested in the specific findings learned through the field-testing process can contact the Home and School Institute for a complete report.

TIPS FOR GOOD RESULTS

1. Write a note or mark the calendar to be sure you remember to do the "recipe." This is your special time together.
2. Pick the time to do the activity together with your child. At school, math may start each day at 9:10. Home teaching is more tuned to the moods of both parent and child. Your activity time can vary from day to day.
3. Read the entire "recipe" carefully. You then know what it is about. Explain to your child what you both will be doing step-by-step.
4. Don't worry about doing anything wrong. Neither you nor your child can do these "recipes" wrong.
5. Start the activity positively. A how-would-you-like-to question may receive a "no" answer from children. Instead try, "Let's do this activity."
6. Believe that your child can "do the job." If he's unsure, remind him of earlier successes. Examples of reminders might be that he swam across the pool even though he was scared. He caught that fish. He went down the high slide at the playground.
7. Don't expect a perfect job. Be sincere in your praise, but don't overdo it. Display your child's work for the rest of the family to enjoy.
8. Use the "recipes" as beginning points. The "recipes" improve as you try them different ways, just as cooking does. Look to the "More Ideas" for ways to make the activity easier or harder to match your child's interest.
9. Use your own imagination and creativity. Ask your children for their ideas.
10. Enjoy! Share your joy about yourself and your children with family and friends.

Families Learning Together
a daily life curriculum

For Children	For Adults
Reading  Mathematics 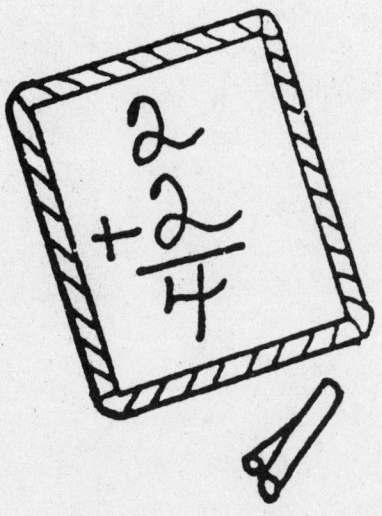	OCCUPATIONAL KNOWLEDGE CONSUMER ECONOMICS COMMUNITY RESOURCES HEALTH CITIZENSHIP

II. INTRODUCING THE "RECIPES"

Here is the collection of **Families Learning Together** "recipes." The "recipes" are divided into four sections:

Reading: Grades K–3
Grades 4–6

Mathematics: Grades K–3
Grades 4–6

In front of each section is a page on which the adult and child learning in each "recipe" is outlined.

The **Blueprint for Family Learning** presents in chart form the way in which the program is built. The major headings show the adult knowledge areas. The math and reading "recipes" at each grade level are indicated in the "houses."

The Blueprint and the section pages are included to help families select the activities in which they are most interested.

For example, a parent interested in health and safety at home with a child in grade 4 interested in reading might select Operation Alert.

Each "recipe" activity contains a consistent set of ingredients. Watch for these symbols:

 This section explains the importance of what you are doing for the child's education and what your child can be expected to learn.

 This section provides additional learning and facts designed to build adult parenting and basic knowledge.

 This section offers tips to parents on how to make the activity work easily.

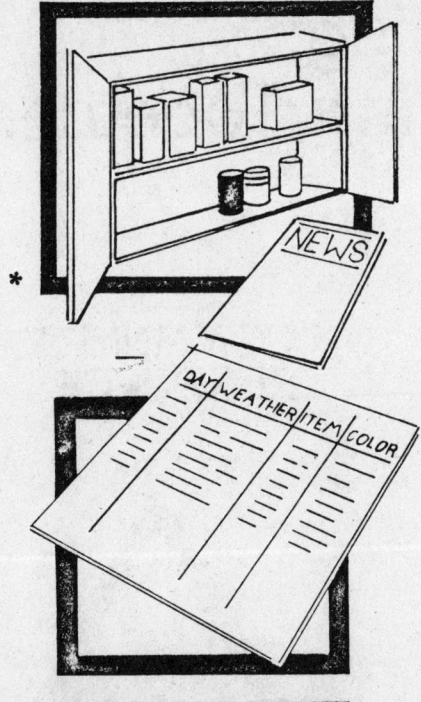

Materials Needed—This section lists the materials needed from the home to do the activity.

Doing It—This is a step-by-step description of how to do the activity.

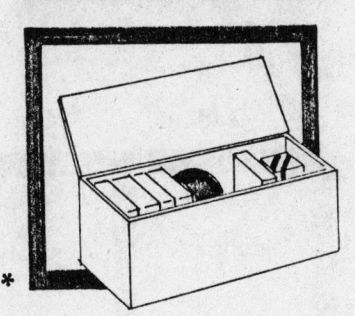

More Ideas—This section offers tips for younger and older children. It includes ideas your family can try in order to meet the special needs of your child.

Reward—This section suggests a special way to tell your child: "You've done a good job."

* The symbols for Materials Needed, Doing It and More Ideas are different for each "recipe." These are examples from the Everything Fits "recipe."

Note: These activities are for both girls and boys. To keep sentences shorter, "he" is used instead of "he or she." What is important is that all children try as many activities as possible.

Curriculum Graphics by Gillian Thompson

Blueprint for Family Learning: Adults and Children Learning Together

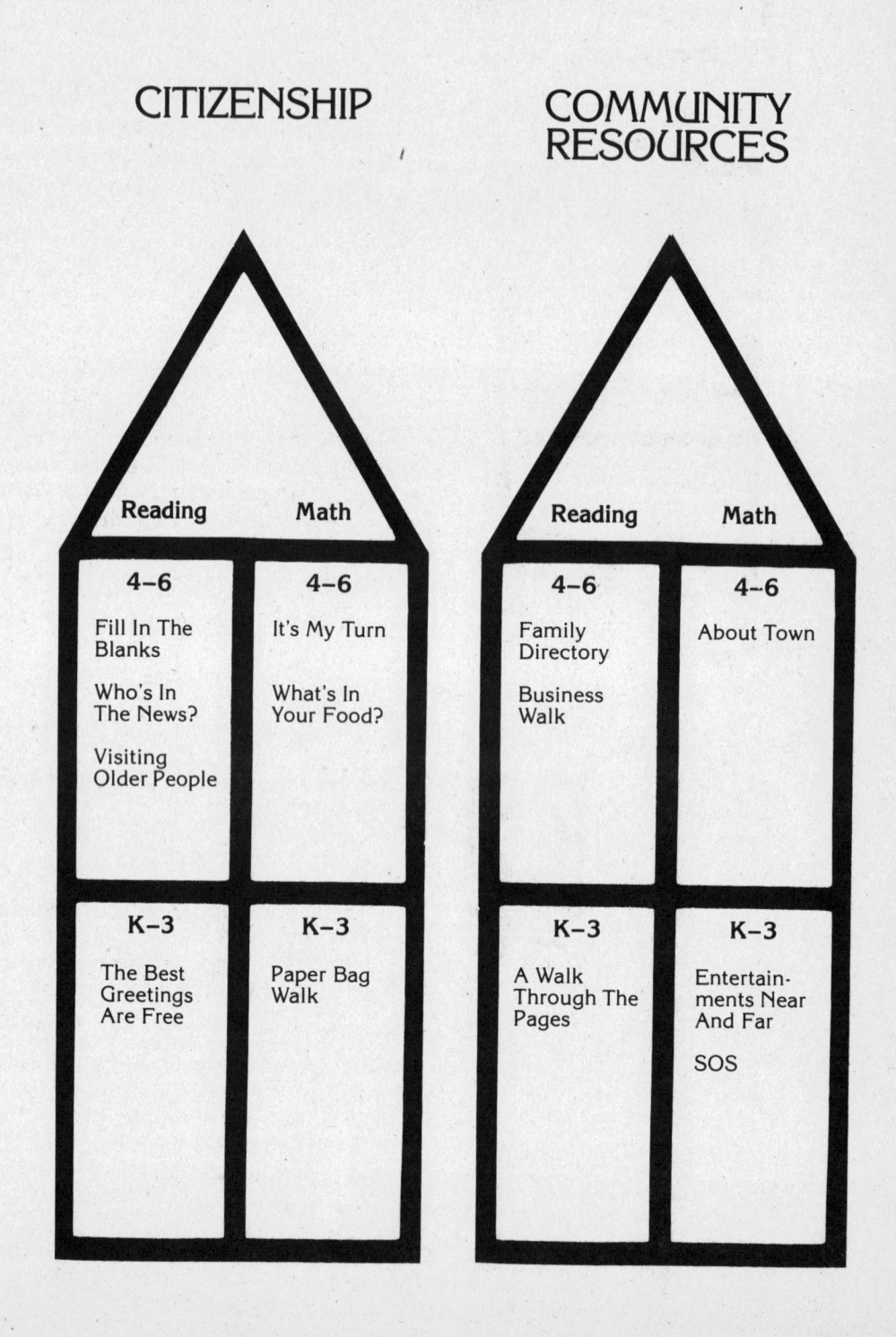

CITIZENSHIP

Reading

4–6

Fill In The Blanks

Who's In The News?

Visiting Older People

K–3

The Best Greetings Are Free

Math

4–6

It's My Turn

What's In Your Food?

K–3

Paper Bag Walk

COMMUNITY RESOURCES

Reading

4–6

Family Directory

Business Walk

K–3

A Walk Through The Pages

Math

4–6

About Town

K–3

Entertainments Near And Far

SOS

CONSUMER ECONOMICS

Reading 4–6
- What Do You Think?
- How Much Is It?

Math 4–6
- Saving And Banking
- Making Money Count
- Prices Going Up
- The Best Buys Have It

Reading K–3
- Water Tour
- Bottom Shelf Shopper

Math K–3
- Food And Money
- Weigh Me

HEALTH

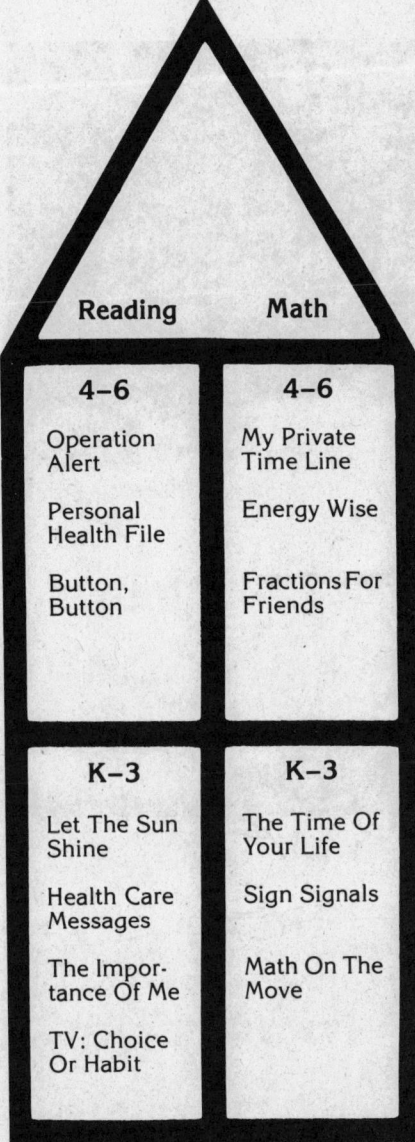

Reading 4–6
- Operation Alert
- Personal Health File
- Button, Button

Math 4–6
- My Private Time Line
- Energy Wise
- Fractions For Friends

Reading K–3
- Let The Sun Shine
- Health Care Messages
- The Importance Of Me
- TV: Choice Or Habit

Math K–3
- The Time Of Your Life
- Sign Signals
- Math On The Move

OCCUPATIONAL KNOWLEDGE

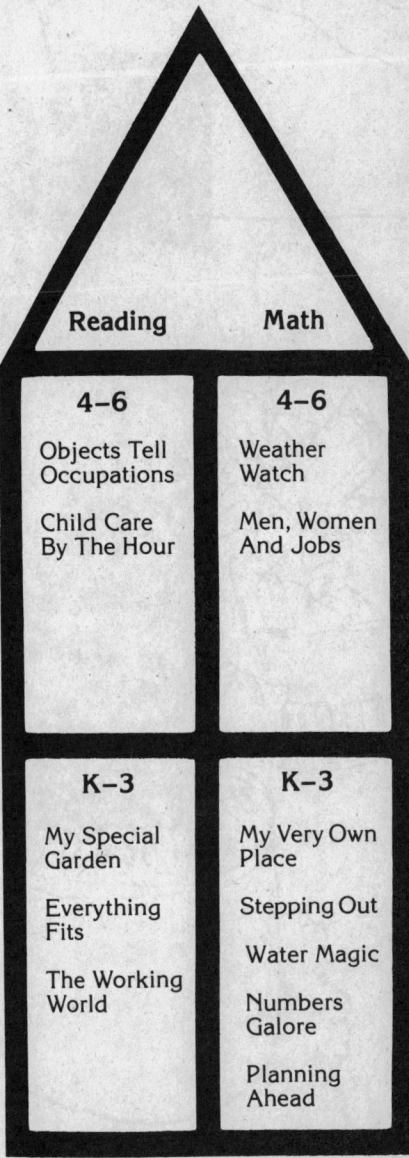

Reading 4–6
- Objects Tell Occupations
- Child Care By The Hour

Math 4–6
- Weather Watch
- Men, Women And Jobs

Reading K–3
- My Special Garden
- Everything Fits
- The Working World

Math K–3
- My Very Own Place
- Stepping Out
- Water Magic
- Numbers Galore
- Planning Ahead

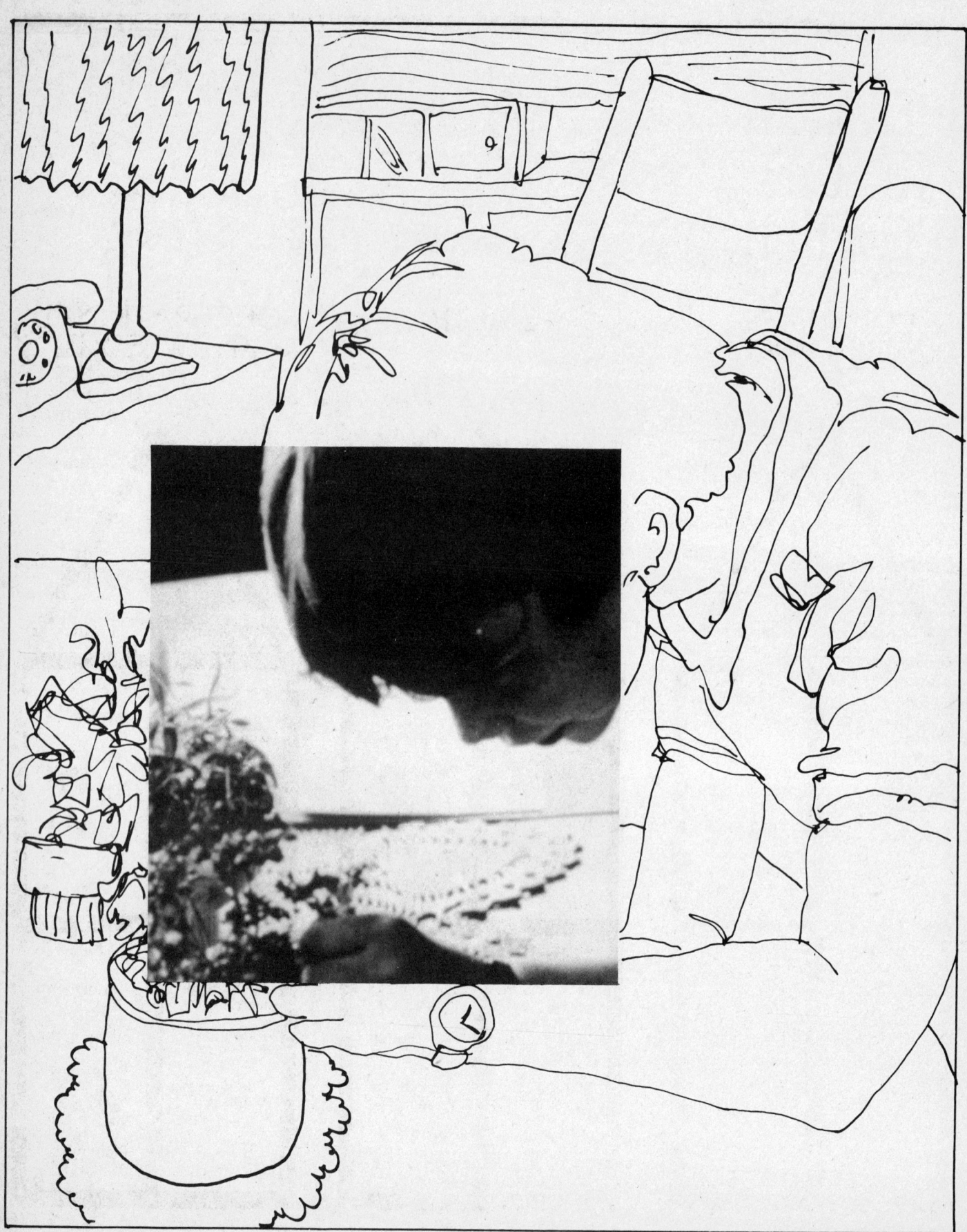

READING: GRADES KINDERGARTEN TO THIRD

The 12 home learning "recipes" in this section are arranged for the children from easiest to hardest.

The listing below gives a special learning for the adults and a special learning for the children in each "recipe."

1. **The Importance of Me**
   Adults learn how important it is for their children to feel good about themselves, to have self-esteem.
   Children learn to think about what they like and what they are like.

2. **The Working World**
   Adults learn about new skills needed for new kinds of jobs.
   Children learn about the many different kinds of jobs that people can do.

3. **My Special Garden**
   Adults learn how important it is for children to have the satisfaction of finishing a job that they have started.
   Children learn to grow their own plants from seeds.

4. **A Walk Through The Pages**
   Adults learn ways to use the telephone directory for information.
   Children learn to improve their observation skills.

5. **Everything Fits**
   Adults learn ways to organize items at home to make everyday tasks easier.
   Children learn how to organize objects together that look alike or have the same use.

6. **Let The Sun Shine**
   Adults learn how to help children have confidence in what they can do.
   Children learn ways to make others feel good.

7. **Bottom Shelf Shopper**
   Adults learn that children who are busy, while parents are shopping do not become bored.
   Children learn the importance of planning in advance by making lists of things to remember.

8. **The Best Greetings Are Free**
   Adults learn how to teach children to be thoughtful by being kind to others.
   Children learn that they can make their own gifts to show their love.

9. **Health Care Messages**
   Adults learn how to help children follow good health and safety habits.
   Children learn to follow personal health routines.

10. **Planning Ahead**
    Adults learn that people dress differently for different occasions.
    Children learn to plan what to wear, so that their clothes are clean and ready to use.

11. **Water Tour**
    Adults learn about how home water use can be conserved.
    Children learn that water costs money and that it should not be wasted.

12. **TV: Choice Or Habit**
    Adults learn about the importance of helping children make television viewing choices.
    Children learn how to regulate their own television.

The Importance Of Me
Making A Poster Life Story
(Autobiography) With Magazine Pictures Or Snapshots

This activity will help children build pride in themselves and in the things they can do.

Learning Together

Children need to have a good self image. This means that they like themselves. It also means that they know their family likes them.

Children who like themselves do better in school. Hobbies help people feel good about themselves.

Did You Know

Adults who do well in their jobs usually had hobbies when they were children. These hobbies might be playing sports or collecting rocks. Hobbies are not a waste of time. They can help children work successfully.

Help To Make This Activity Work

Make yourself a poster too! You help your child when you work right along with him.

Talk about your interests. Tell about your hobbies when you were a child. Show these on the poster.

Step 1-Materials

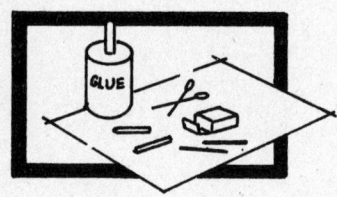

A large sheet of paper, posterboard or cardboard
   (Grocery bags can be cut and taped/pasted
     together to make a large size piece of paper.)
Collect old magazines. Be sure they can be cut up.
Family snapshots, if available, (those you have
   extras of or don't mind using).

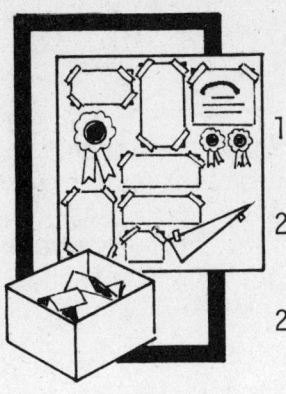

Step 2-Doing It

1. Together, look through magazines. Find pictures that tell about what the whole family has done.

2. Find pictures of the things your child likes such as pets, foods, and clothes.

2. Work with him to cut out pictures and arrange them on a large sheet of paper. This will be the poster.

3. Magazines are fine. If you have extra snapshots, use them. Perhaps you can both choose some pictures to add to the poster.

4. Paste the pictures on the paper.

5. Write a few words on the poster. Those words can tell about the pictures. You can write the words for a younger child. Examples: "Look at me at 4 years old!" "See the picture of my brother."

Step 3-More Ideas

Leave space at the bottom of the poster for adults to write nice things. For example, "This is a pretty dress." "Look at the fish that was caught."

Take turns and make poster life stories of other family members.

Draw pictures of other members of the family and display these about the house.

Put up a bulletin board in your child's room. You child can tack up cards he receives, art work, pictures of interest, a calendar and snapshots.

Step 4-Reward

Hang the poster in a special place for all to see and enjoy. Good places are the front door or the refrigerator door.

The Working World
"Reading" Pictures Of Workers

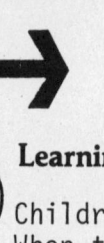

This activity will teach children about the many jobs (careers and occupations) that people can choose. Boys and girls will have a wide choice of jobs when they grow up.

Learning Together

Children should learn to "read" pictures and look for details. When they read pictures, they can answer these questions. What is happening? Who do I see? What are they doing? Why are they doing it? Have I ever seen this happening in real life? Children love pictures. Picture reading helps to strengthen children's ability to understand what is written. This activity can teach children to read in an informal at-home way.

Did You Know

Jobs are increasing and changing. A century ago the United States had 300 times more blacksmiths than electricians. Today, there are 50 times more electricians than blacksmiths. A hundred years ago people used horses for transportation. Blacksmiths were needed. Now we drive cars.

Machines and technology (the science of industry) change the kinds of jobs people do. Machines can take over jobs that used to be done by hand. Farmers now plow their fields with tractors instead of a hand plow and a horse. Most families don't wash clothes by hand anymore. They use washing machines.

Help To Make This Activity Work

Look through some magazines or newspapers. Choose those that show pictures of workers. Look for farmers, plumbers, construction workers and medical workers.

Step 1-Materials

Magazine or magazine sections of the newspaper
Scissors
Tape

Step 2-Doing It

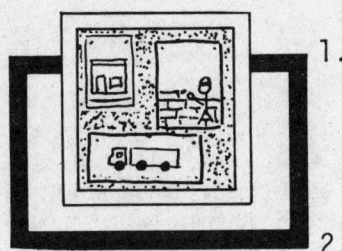

1. Talk about the jobs that people do. Talk about the kinds of work your own family members do. They may be plumbers, waitresses or doctors. Talk about where people work and about the clothes or uniforms workers wear. Talk about some of the tools workers use, such as hammers and drills.

2. Together, look through magazines to find pictures of people doing many kinds of work.

3. Help read the pictures by asking questions. "What kind of work is he doing?" "Why is she dressed the way she is?" "Have you ever seen a person doing this job?"

4. Ask your child to look through magazines to choose three or four pictures he likes. Cut them out. Ask him what jobs he would like to do when he grows up.

5. Together pick a special place to keep the pictures so you may both look at them often.

Step 3-More Ideas

Talk together about what kinds of jobs your child might like to do. Ask what he wants to do when he grows up. Have him explain why he wants to do the job he chooses.

Ask him to make up a story about one or two of his pictures. Decide which one of you will write the story. Tape the story to the picture. Help read the story.

Tape a piece of paper to the picture. Let your second or third grader write his own words under the pictures (captions). Help with spelling if necessary.

Step 4-Reward

A favorite picture of a worker can become a jigsaw puzzle. Glue or paste the picture to stiff paper or cardboard. Mark several dark lines over the picture. Follow these lines to cut the puzzle.

If you want the puzzle to be easy, mark only a few lines. To make the puzzle harder, mark and cut more lines. You can make as many pieces as you want. Keep the pieces of each puzzle together in a separate envelope.

These puzzles can help your child think about jobs. You can also make puzzles to give as gifts.

My Special Garden
Planting Seeds Indoors or Outdoors

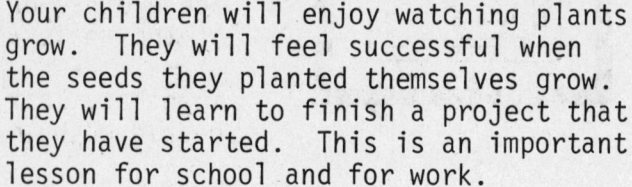

Your children will enjoy watching plants grow. They will feel successful when the seeds they planted themselves grow. They will learn to finish a project that they have started. This is an important lesson for school and for work.

Learning Together

Children look at objects to see likenesses and differences. This helps them learn how to compare and to sort objects. Sorting objects is a lot like sorting alphabet letters. Knowing differences among alphabet letters is an important reading skill.

Children are born with special talents in music, art, science, etc. They must develop strengths of character to use these special talents. These strengths include sticking to a task (perseverance) and reaching out to new challenges. Working hard on a project (for example, making a garden) helps develop these skills at home.

Did You Know

Flowers have their own built-in alarm clocks. These clocks are set to go off at special times. Scientists have learned the secret of setting the clocks to make plants grow faster. The electric lights in greenhouses are set to make more nights and days. Flowers are made to bloom ahead of time so people can have flowers from florists in the middle of winter.

Help To Make This Activity Work

When both of you plant, you double your chances that some seeds will sprout.

Begin saving some beans and seeds from your kitchen. Orange and grapefruit seeds are some of the best for indoor planting. Beans and radishes grow well both inside and outside. A good rule is to plant these seeds about ½ inch below the soil. Show your child how to use the ruler to measure this.

If you begin your garden in winter, you can start seedlings indoors. Tomatoes and green peppers are good for this purpose.

Step 1-Materials

Two or three packets of seeds: saved or bought
Two or three small pots or milk cartons
A large, flat surface, water, soil
A sunny window sill, slips of paper, pencil, ruler

Step 2-Doing It

1. Buy 2 or 3 packets of seeds or use the seeds you have saved.

2. Empty a few seeds on the table beside each packet.

3. Ask your child to look at the seeds. He can put them together. Look at (compare) the seeds--their size and color. Feel how hard they are. Talk about the differences.

4. Help fill each pot with two inches of soil. Use the ruler to measure. In warm weather, you can plant outside.

5. Plant a few seeds in each pot. Together read the directions on the seed packet. Talk about what you have to do to be sure the seeds grow.

6. Place the pots on a sunny window sill.

7. Help copy the names of the seeds on slips of paper. Put a slip of paper near each pot.

8. Each day water the pots. Watch for the seeds to begin to sprout. Seeds grow slowly. It will take about 10 days to see them begin to grow.

Step 3-More Ideas

A second or third grader can keep a plant "diary." Record the little changes that you both see in the plants each day. A kindergartner or first grader can tell you what he sees.

You may want to start an herb garden on your window sill. You can use these herbs when you cook.

Step 4-Reward

Share one or more of your home grown plants with a sick friend, senior citizen, or a nursing home.

Plants have a way of saying, "We love you and we care."

A Walk Through The Pages
Finding Information In Magazines And Catalogs

This activity will help children use magazines or catalogs to find pictures that show similar things. The pictures go into groups or "categories." They might be pictures of animals, foods, toys, etc.

Learning Together

Children need certain basic skills to find information. First, they need experience in looking through books and magazines for information. They can put this information into areas that go together. This activity is called "grouping."

Using magazines to find material for grouping builds children's skills. They will be able to find information as they need it.

Did You Know

You can save time checking for product information by looking in the yellow pages for the type of product you wish to purchase. Go down the list of suppliers to find store locations near you. Call before going to the store. You can find out the cost of the item you want. You can also find out if the item is in stock. This comparison shopping by telephone can save you time and money.

Help To Make This Activity Work

Before you begin, be sure that you have magazines and catalogs with pictures that interest your child.

Step 1-Materials

Old magazines or catalogs containing pictures of
    foods, toys, and so on.
Yellow pages of telephone book
Pen/pencil
Paper
Scissors

Step 2-Doing It

1. Tell your child that you are going to play a game. You will use magazines and catalogs to find pictures.

2. Find different pictures of the same things. Find several pictures of trucks, cars, food, cats, dogs, toys, etc. Cut these out. Glue each picture on a piece of paper.

3. Ask your child to play the game by putting the pictures together that go together. Trucks go together; cats go together, etc.

   This game can be played many times. Add new pictures as needed.

4. Ask your child to tell you why he grouped the pictures as he did. Does he see the likenesses and differences among the items? This activity helps prepare your child for better reading. It builds children's observation skills.

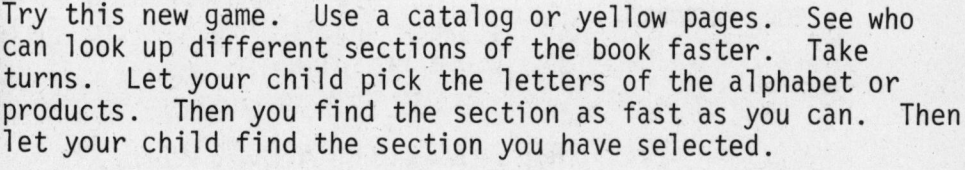

Step 3-More Ideas

Try this new game. Use a catalog or yellow pages. See who can look up different sections of the book faster. Take turns. Let your child pick the letters of the alphabet or products. Then you find the section as fast as you can. Then let your child find the section you have selected.

Call out a product or service from a catalog. Let your child tell the letter of the alphabet with which it begins. For example, you might say "toys" and he will say "t." Take turns.

Step 4-Reward

Your child can cut pictures from magazines to make his own catalog. In the A section he can cut out all of the animals that he finds. In the B section he can cut out all of the bicycles that he finds. He can keep adding other sections. Encourage him to use his imagination in putting this book together.

Children who read can make a book of words. This can be their very own dictionary.

Everything Fits
Arranging Kitchen Shelves

This activity will help children learn how to put things into order. This will help you by organizing your kitchen cans and containers.

Learning Together

Children should learn to put things together that are alike. When they put things that are alike together they are organizing. Children need these skills in order to read and write better.

Children learn to organize best by handling objects. Help them by getting practice in organizing at home. For example, people read by organizing sounds and symbols (the alphabet). People write by organizing ideas.

Did You Know

Studies show that arranging your spices in ABC (alphabetical) order saves time. Few homes ever have enough storage space. One secret to good housekeeping is well organized storage space. Organization helps to give you more space.

Help To Make This Activity Work

Pick a low shelf that your child can reach. Help him arrange things so that you can find them easily.

Maybe your shelves are already organized. Then begin with his own bedroom drawers or shelves. Together, you can label the outside of the drawers. For example, "Socks," "Underwear," "Sweaters." If he has only a large drawer or two, use cardboard to make sections. Then use two or three labels on each section.

Step 1-Materials

Cupboard or cabinet shelves with cans, boxes, etc.
Newspaper to spread on floor for a good working space

Step 2-Doing It

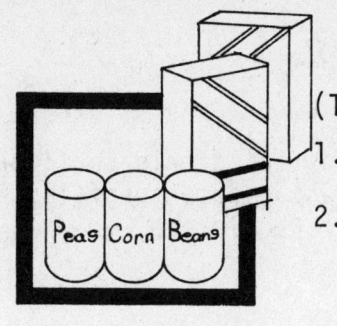

(The basic steps are the same for organizing any activity.)

1. Start with one shelf.

2. Talk about the best way to organize the shelf. Which would be more helpful?

    Organize cans by size? Put all short ones together, all fat ones together, all tall ones together?

    Organize by food groups? Put all vegetables together, all fruits together?

    Organize by the type of containers? Put all boxes together, all cans together?

3. Let your child know how well he is doing. Keep the good words coming!

Step 3-More Ideas

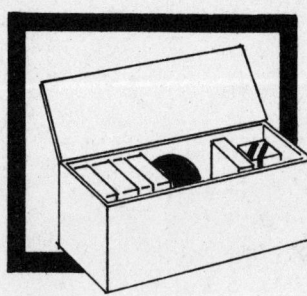

Your child can also organize his own things, such as a toy box or homework supplies.

Use a bedroom drawer and a laundry load of your child's clothes. Your child can sort these items.

He can help the family by organizing the linen closet. He can put together shoes in the bottom of closets.

To help the younger child, put pictures from magazines on the front of the drawer. You might use pictures of socks, sweaters, underwear.

Step 4-Reward

Once the cupboard, closet or drawers have been reorganized, put a label on it. "This Cupboard was arranged by Billy."

These new arrangements should help the family. Your child will feel proud to help his family.

Let The Sun Shine
Letting Others Know How Much We Love Them

This activity builds children's confidence. They can feel they have some special skills. They can make other people feel good.

Learning Together

Children should learn to be considerate of others. They need to practice being helpful to others. They also need to learn to give encouragement and help to others. Special daily notes which say "something nice" are a good start. Think of what your child does well and share these thoughts.

Did You Know

Children who feel confident will try to do more things.

When children feel confident, they get along better with other people. A sense of confidence allows children to become independent and emotionally strong. Emotionally healthy people become more involved in the community.

Help To Make This Activity Work

Help your child develop confidence by giving encouragement. Avoid general statements like "You're nice." Instead be specific, "You're a great cook of fried eggs," or "You are a good bicycle rider."

Step 1-Materials

Pen, pencil or marker
Paper

Step 2-Doing It

1. Tell your child that each day, for three days, you and he will send each other notes. Each note will be a special message. The message will say something nice.

2. The "something nice" must be something true that you noticed about him or that he noticed about you. It might be, "You have a nice smile." It might be "Your dinner last night was very good." Or "I like the way you cooked the chicken."

3. If your child does not write yet, he can dictate his messages to you. Then you can read your own notes aloud to him.

4. Children who can read and write will enjoy expressing their feelings. They will like thinking, "What nice thing shall I say?"

5. Decide on a place to exchange daily notes. You can put them on the refrigerator, in lunch bags or at the dinner table.

Step 3-More Ideas

Use special or colored paper for these notes. This makes the activity more fun. Encourage your child to keep on sending these nice messages. This is an easy way to make people happy.

Step 4-Reward

Ask a surprise "mystery guest" to send your child a nice note. It might be a message from a best friend, from grandparents, or from a neighbor.

Bottom Shelf Shopper
Making A Grocery List And Shopping Together

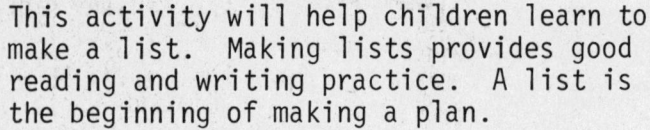

This activity will help children learn to make a list. Making lists provides good reading and writing practice. A list is the beginning of making a plan.

Knowing how to plan helps children organize their day. Planning is important for daily living and for school success.

Learning Together

A grocery list helps you plan what to buy. It can save you money when shopping for food. By knowing what is needed at home, spur-of-the-moment (impulse) buying can be reduced. You also can avoid returning to the store for items that you forgot.

Did You Know

There are things you can do at the grocery store so that children can help while you both shop.

With children who are not yet reading, do this activity: As you go down each aisle, ask, "Will we find something on our list here?" The children keep busy looking. This will help avoid their asking for "junk food" or other items you don't need.

Let young readers check off items on your list. If there are several sizes of a product, see if they can find the biggest and the smallest. Ask them to find two cans that are the same. Show them which one costs less. In this way they can start being wise shoppers.

Help To Make This Activity Work

Children feel especially close to parents who listen to and use their ideas. For example, your child could choose a food from each of the main food groups. These groups are vegetables, fruits, meats, dairy products and grain products. He might choose one bread product, one dairy product and one fruit. Be sure to write the choices on your shopping list.

Step 1-Materials

Paper, cardboard (can be cut from boxes)
Pencil or crayons

Step 2-Doing It

1. Think about what you want to eat in the next few days. Then let the child help plan and make up the grocery list.

2. To make the list, you and your child can check your shelves and your refrigerator. Check the items you have on hand and those you need from the store. Make a list of the items you need from the store.

3. After you make the list, both of you can check it to be sure you have written down everything you need.

4. At the store, put your child in charge of finding items that do not break, such as boxes or cans.

5. Ask your child to check the bottom shelves. As a game, count how many items from your list are on the bottom shelves. If nothing on your list is on the bottom shelf, then together you can look on the upper shelves.

6. Put the items that you've both agreed to buy onto the check-out counter.

Step 3-More Ideas

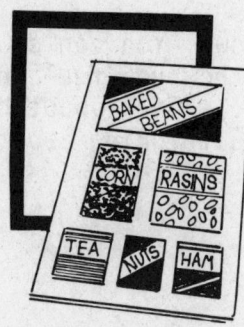

Make "Picture Lists" for a kindergartner or first grader who doesn't read yet. Here's how to do it. Paste five labels from items you regularly buy onto a piece of cardborad. (For example, labels from tomato soup or bread.) Ask your child to match the labels on his picture list with items in the store.

Bring to the store any "cents-off" coupons for products you want. Your young reader can look for products that match these coupons. Figure out how much money you've saved. This gives your child math practice.

Step 4-Reward

You might allow your child to keep a little of the money received from "cents-off" coupons you've used. He might save money from soda pop bottles or cans that are returned for a refund. Using this money, he can choose a small inexpensive item for himself. Help him spend this money wisely.

The Best Greetings Are Free
Sharing Thoughtfulness Through Greeting Cards

This activity will help children practice reading and writing skills. It will also teach them to be thoughtful of others.

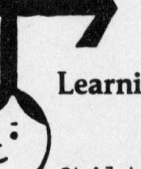

Learning Together

Children should see that reading and writing can be used for fun activities at home. Making pretty birthday cards, get well cards or "thinking of you" cards gives them practice in these skills. A handmade card pleases the person who gets it. It also saves money.

Did You Know

Children can be helped to become more giving. They can learn to be kind to others. It helps when they see their parents and other adults being kind.

It also helps when they see other children helping people. They become more kind and considerate themselves. Rewarding a child when he is kind is a way to increase this good behavior.

Help To Make This Activity Work

Make a greeting card for someone you know. You can do this while your child makes his. Talk about how you feel when you get a card from a friend or relative. Talk about how you feel when you know another person is thinking about you.

Step 1-Materials

White or colored paper
Crayons or markers
Pieces of scrap materials--yarn, fabric, buttons and so on.
Glue

Step 2-Doing It

1. Together, decide who will get a card. Does someone need cheering up? Is a friend having a birthday?

2. Help your child fold the paper.

3. Make a design on the cover of the card. Your child can glue scraps of paper or materials on the front of the card. He might color it. An older child might write a poem on the card. It can be his own or one that he copied.

4. Now print the message on the inside of the card. If your child doesn't write yet, help him. This message can be short such as "I love you!" It can be a longer message such as "Have a Happy Birthday!" or "Have a good day!"

5. Help your child address the card and put it in the mail.

Step 3-More Ideas

The child can make several kinds of greeting cards at one time. Then he will have cards ready for all kinds of holidays. If an event comes up, he will be prepared.

He can make a box of greeting cards to give as a gift. An older person will enjoy getting three or four cards that can be used to send to friends and relatives.

Step 4-Reward

Make a greeting card to give to your child. It might say something like "You're a great artist!" or "You're a great helper!"

35

Health Care Messages
Reminding Children Without Nagging

It is possible to build children's good health habits without nagging them. In this activity, children will read your reminder messages about things they must do to stay healthy. The messages can be in words and pictures.

Learning Together

Children should learn about good health habits. There are basic rules needed to maintain healthy bodies. You can tell them about these rules. If you get a cut, be sure to clean it with soap and water. This helps to avoid infection. If you get very wet in a rainstorm, change to dry clothes as soon as possible. This prevents your body from getting chilled.

Many children need to be reminded to comb their hair and brush their teeth. They must be reminded to put on their boots and button their coats. Using written reminders helps them become more independent and responsible. It also saves your energy. They can read the written message and do what it says.
If they can't read yet, you can draw a simple picture message.

Did You Know

To maintain fitness, we need to be active. Here are three simple ways.

1. Stretch all over. This makes your body more flexible.

2. Stand up as often as you can during the day. Health experts say that two hours of standing each day is good for you. This strengthens bones. It helps blood circulation.

3. Walk briskly even if only for three minutes. This is good for your heart.

Help To Make This Activity Work

You should place the messages near the places your child will do them. The messages should be at his eye level. "Please wash your hands" would be a message near the sink. The picture message can show hands, soap and sink.

36

Step 1-Materials

Two to four slips of paper
Pencil/crayon

Step 2-Doing It

1. Ask your child, "What do I remind you to do most often?" These reminders might be: dress warmly and wear boots when it rains. Tie shoelaces tightly. Clean your room. Keep the stairs clear. Choose three ideas that are important to your child's health and safety. Then say, "I remind you because I love you."

2. Write a simple note. Use as few words as possible. Write the reminders in big letters on each sheet. Here are some samples:

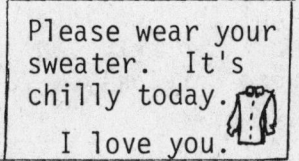

| Please wear your sweater. It's chilly today. I love you. | Please brush your teeth with up and down strokes. I love you. | Please wear your boots when it rains. I love you. |

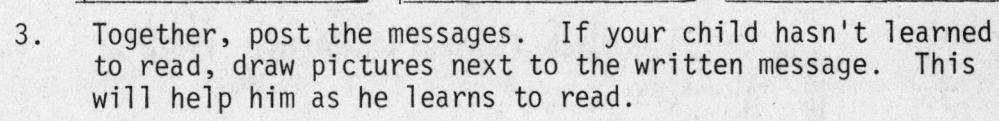

3. Together, post the messages. If your child hasn't learned to read, draw pictures next to the written message. This will help him as he learns to read.

Step 3-More Ideas

Children can write messages or draw pictures to remind you of things. Let them make reminder notes before you go on errands together.

Step 4-Reward

Children can post reminder messages for the family. The refrigerator is a great place for family "care" messages.

Planning Ahead
Making Decisions

Children will be able to make decisions about the next day. They will choose what to wear. You can make a note of their choice.

Learning Together

Children need to learn how to plan for their daily needs. They must make decisions about tomorrow. Children have to be taught that we don't live only for today. Our tomorrows can be better if we plan for them. Good management depends on planning ahead.

Did You Know

You can dress to fit the occasion just as you use different tools for different jobs. Jeans are fine for play and recreation. Usually they are not right for job interviews unless the job requires work clothes. On job interviews, it's wise to dress carefully. You should appear neat and well groomed.

Help To Make This Activity Work

Start with a major piece of clothing. This can be pants or skirt. Then try to choose the other pieces of clothing to match. It is a good idea to try to wear clothes that go together. Sports clothes go with other sports clothes. Dressy clothes go together.

Step 1-Materials

Young child's clothing
Pen/pencil
Paper

Step 2-Doing It

1. Before your child goes to bed for the night, ask him to think about which clothes he should wear tomorrow. Have him think about what he will be doing. Will he be at school or playing in the neighborhood? Has it been cold or hot? Will there be snow or rain? Talk about the weather prediction for tomorrow.

2. Together, think about the clothes he will wear tomorrow. This may be a choice between a sweater or a coat. It depends on the weather.

3. Make a note of the clothing you both choose. Ask your child to read the note to you. Help him read the words he doesn't understand.

4. Let him check to see if the clothes he needs are clean and ready.

5. Post the note at your child's eye level. Put it near his closet or his mirror. Praise him the next day as he chooses the items he's picked.

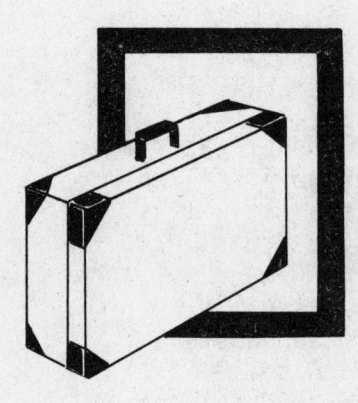

Step 3-More Ideas

Have your child make up sets of clothing. Use pictures of clothing cut from magazines. He can plan clothes for a vacation, a visit to a relative or a camping trip. He can pack the paper clothes in a shoe box. It will be like packing a suitcase.

Are you going on a family trip? Allow your child to help pack his suitcase.

Step 4-Reward

Every child would enjoy having his very own calendar. A calendar helps a child look ahead and think about tomorrow. Your child can draw or write a note about tomorrow's weather on his calendar. Calendars can be made, bought or obtained free. Put your child's name in big print at the top of his special calendar.

Water Tour
Conserving Water At Home

This activity will teach children about the ways a family uses water at home. They will also think of ways to save on the amount of water a family uses.

Learning Together

Children should realize that water is a natural resource we need to conserve. They must also learn that water is not free. Water costs the family money. Homes are billed by the city for the water used.

If the home has a pump system for water, then the homeowner must take care of the system. A pump system, which runs by electricity, costs money every time water is used.

The less water a family uses, the more money the family saves. Families need to find ways to save on the amount of water used.

Did You Know

The average person uses 3000 gallons of water a month. A standard five foot bathtub is filled with 50 gallons of water. That's a lot. It's even more if your house has leaky faucets.

In one day a dripping faucet can waste 170 gallons of water. A running drip can waste 600 gallons of water in one day. A small steady flow from a leak can waste 2500 gallons of water a day. It is possible, even easy, to fix leaky faucets. One publication that tells how is <u>Simple Home Repairs...inside</u>. You can get it from the U. S. Department of Agriculture Extension Service. Call your local Cooperative Extension Service for "how-to-get-it" information.

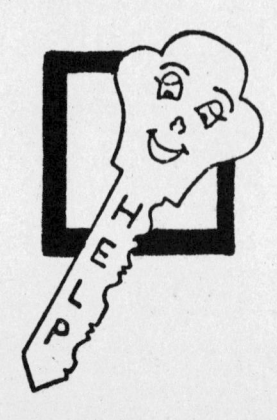

Help To Make This Activity Work

Before you begin this activity, think of all the ways your family uses water. Ask your child to think of where the family uses water. Combine your lists.

Step 1-Materials

Paper
Pen/pencil

Step 2-Doing It

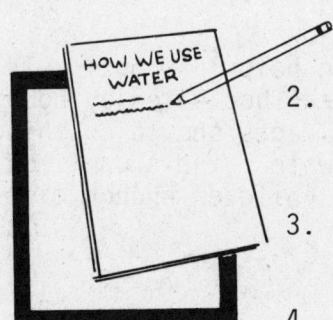

1. Go through each room of the house with your child. In each room ask how the family uses water there. If there's a faucet, listen for a drip.

2. Write down what your child says in simple words. For example: "We use water to wash the floor, to water the plants, to wash the dishes."

3. Read the list to your child after you have both finished. If your child can read, let him read the list to you.

4. Talk about how water costs money. Ask him to help you think of a few ways to save water. Let him know this will save money. For example, use less water in the bathtub. Fix leaky faucets. Use water from a defrosted refrigerator to water plants. Put a brick in the tank of the toilet to use less water.

5. Write these ideas down as you and your child think of them. Read them to your child. Let him read them to you.

Step 3-More Ideas

Take an "electricity tour" through your house. List ways you now use electricity. Try to think of as many as you can. Talk about ways to save on electric bills.

Step 4-Reward

Start using the "water saving" ideas you and your child have listed. Make a list of water saving ideas to post on the refrigerator. Show it to friends who come to your home. See if they can add ideas or if they would like to try your ideas.

TV: Choice Or Habit
Making Choices About What To Watch And When

This activity will teach children to use free time wisely. The whole family will think about choices for TV watching. The family will be aware of time spent before the "tube."

Learning Together

It's important for children to have help in choosing TV programs. Children need time to read books, enjoy hobbies, and play outdoors. Children of all ages should do things themselves. They should not just watch others on TV do them. Watching too much TV does not give children enough time to do other activities.

Did You Know

Children between the ages of 2 and 11 watch nearly 26 hours of television a week. That's about 4 hours a day. Teenagers watch about 22 hours a week. People say this is too much time spent just sitting and watching.

Help To Make This Activity Work

Read the TV schedule with your child. Ask him which programs he wants to watch. Talk about why one program might be a better choice than the other. It may be the viewing hours. It may be what the show is about. Tell your child what you think about certain programs. Decide together how many hours a day you both will watch TV. You may want to set time limits.

Step 1-Materials

TV set
Daily or weekly TV guide (find these in the daily paper)
Pencil
Paper
Ruler

Step 2-Doing It

1. Make a simple chart with your child like the one below. Read the TV schedule to him or let him read it.

2. Ask your child to write down his choices on the TV Plan. If he can't write yet, have him say the words to you and you fill in the chart.

3. After your child makes his chart, make one for yourself. Let your child help you.

4. Post the charts in a special place near the TV set. Put a pencil on a string by it. Keeping a list of the shows you watch will be easy.

5. For at least three days, fill in the charts with the programs you both have watched.

6. Be on the lookout for too much TV watching.

TV Plan

DATE	TIME	PROGRAM NAME	CHANNEL

Step 3-More Ideas

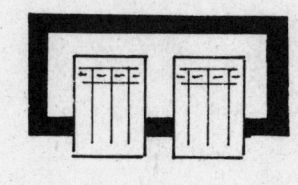

Use the daily or weekly TV guide in the newspaper. Together circle the programs your family will watch. Your child can circle the programs with one colored crayon. You circle your programs with a different colored crayon.

Make other charts. Your child can list or ask you to list how he spends his time. How much time does your child sleep or do homework? How much time does he have for jobs around the house or in the neighborhood? How much time does he play with friends outside the home and talk on the telephone?

Step 4-Reward

Decide with your child on a reward for keeping to the TV time limit for at least 3 days. It could be something needed for a hobby or other favorite activity. It could be going on a family picnic or to a baseball game.

The best reward is that each family member will have more time to play, learn and be together.

44

MATHEMATICS: GRADES KINDERGARTEN TO THIRD

The 12 home learning "recipes" in this section are arranged for the children from easiest to hardest.

The listing below gives a special learning for the adults and a special learning for the children in each "recipe."

1. **Sign Signals**
   Adults learn how to teach children about traffic safety to prevent accidents.
   Children learn to read traffic signs.

2. **Numbers Galore**
   Adults learn the importance of math skills for good jobs.
   Children learn to feel comfortable using numbers.

3. **Math On The Move**
   Adults learn how to begin a program of home health care through exercise.
   Children learn to do exercise and do math at the same time.

4. **Paper Bag Walk**
   Adults learn that what an individual does can make a whole community better.
   Children learn that sharing is important for good citizenship.

5. **The Time Of Our Lives**
   Adults learn about immunizations for their family.
   Children learn about using their time wisely. They get practice in budgeting time.

6. **Food And Money**
   Adults learn about how to save money when buying food.
   Children learn about "unit pricing" and math abbreviations on food packages.

7. **Stepping Out**
   Adults learn about ways to compare and estimate measurements.
   Children learn about ways to measure using parts of their bodies.

8. **Water Magic**
   Adults learn ways to teach science in everyday life.
   Children learn about and experiment with water in its many forms.

9. **Weigh Me**
   Adults learn about the metric system of measurement.
   Children learn how to use scales and to work with fractions.

10. **Entertainments Near And Far**
    Adults learn more about their community and about recreation places near home.
    Children learn how to chart and record activities they can do with their family.

11. **My Very Own Place**
    Adults learn how to keep and file important family records.
    Children learn to organize their own possessions.

12. **SOS**
    Adults learn to help their children handle an emergency using the help available in the community.
    Children learn how to find and use emergency telephone numbers.

Sign Signals
Colors And Shapes That Keep Us Safe

This activity will help children learn to read and to understand signs. Even if they can't always read a sign, they can learn what it says. They can "read" its familiar shape and color.

Learning Together

Children should notice that all signs saying the same thing have the same shape and color. For example, all "stop" signs are red and have eight sides (octagonal). Children who can read signs will be safer as they go out in their community. They will also be able to recognize familiar signs that tell when they are near home, in case they get lost.

Mathematics is different from arithmetic. Arithmetic is counting and measuring. Mathematics is a way of organizing and looking at the world. Looking at shapes and seeing their likenesses and differences is important in math.

Did You Know

Over half of all traffic accidents near houses happen to children under the age of 11. Crossing a street at an intersection is hard for younger children. Children have to learn to look both ways for traffic. Then they must decide when it is safe to cross. Children should learn never to step off a curb without checking all directions, even if they are crossing with a traffic light.

It can help children if you walk with them through the neighborhood while you are teaching them the rules and signals. Watch what they do. Then, let them lead you on the walk and tell you the rules.

Help To Make This Activity Work

If you have time, take a practice walk or drive alone before taking your child out. Then you will know beforehand which streets have more signs and which are the more dangerous intersections.

Step 1-Materials

Street signs
Store signs
All kinds of signs

Step 2-Doing It

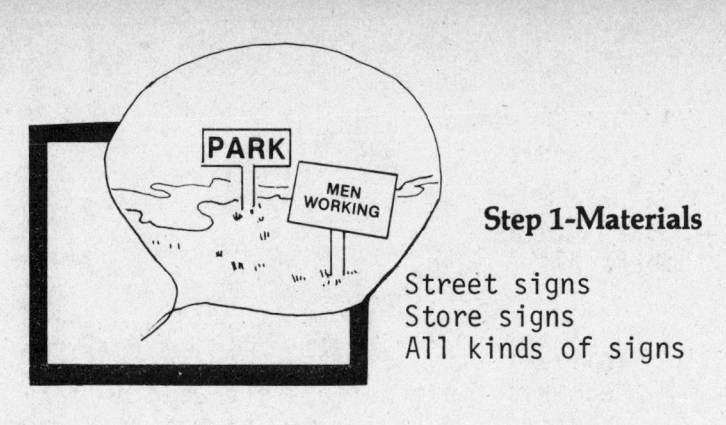

1. Walk with your child or drive through your community.

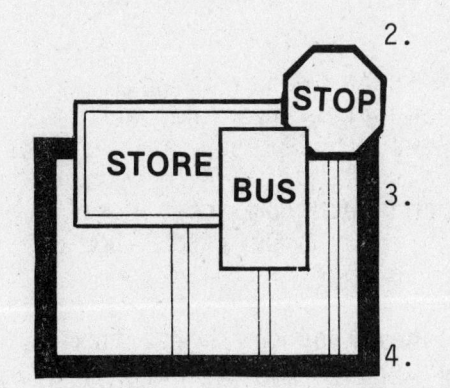

2. Point out the many signs you see. Which are the signs for safety? What do the other signs tell you? For example, bus, yield, walk, caution are some signs you will see.

3. Talk about the shape and color of each sign. Point out signs that are round, square, rectangular, diamond-shaped or triangular. Count how many of each sign that you both see.

4. After your trip, both of you can try to remember how many times you saw a certain sign. For example, "I think I saw a sign that said Walk 3 times. How many times did you see it?"

5. Try to remember where you both saw the different signs. For example, "I think I saw the sign 'Slow, Children Playing' on the street in front of the park."

Step 3-More Ideas

Look through old magazines and newspapers to find pictures of signs. Help cut them out and paste them on a sheet of paper. Take this paper with you when you are driving in the car or riding on a bus. Help your child look for signs that are like the ones you have cut out.

Step 4-Reward

Help your child make a few signs to put up in his bedroom or study area. For example, CHILD AT WORK, EXIT, KNOCK BEFORE ENTERING, PLEASE KEEP OUT. Encourage your child to make up his very own signs.

Numbers Galore
Seeing Numbers All Around Us

This activity will teach children to recognize that numbers are used on many objects. They will be able to read these numbers. Children can learn to feel confident about numbers and math.

Learning Together

Numbers play a very important part in our daily lives. Numbers are used to make a family budget. They are used in weather reports and in sports news.

Children should know how to write and read numbers. Most elementary school children learn to read numbers to 1,000 (one thousand).

Finding numbers at home and in the neighborhood helps them understand that using numbers is a part of day-to-day living.

Did You Know

There is more employment available for a person with high school and college math skills. A survey has shown that college graduates trained in mathematics start at higher salaries. Good math skills give a young person better chances for getting a job and for getting higher wages.

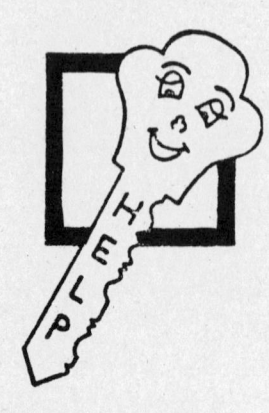

Help To Make This Activity Work

Collect some magazines, newspapers and mail advertisements. Use the numbers in them to show your child what numbers look like and what they are named. Look for big numbers that will stretch your child's imagination. Try to find a number with many zeros in it.

Step 1-Materials

On the first day, find numbers on objects found in the home.

On other days, find numbers on objects in the yard, in the car and in the neighborhood.

Step 2-Doing It

1. Talk to your child about numbers. Ask him where and when he uses numbers.

2. Together, take a trip through the house. See how many things you can find that use numbers. Look for objects such as clocks, pages in books, the electric and gas meters. Look at the dials of washers and dryers. Look at the insides of shoes and on clothing tags. Look at box and can labels, the telephone and calendars.

3. As you find numbers, ask your child to repeat them. If a number has two digits such as 31, ask him to say both numbers separately (three and one). Then ask him to "read" the number (thirty-one). Help him to understand that as numbers get larger, the names of numbers change.

4. On another day, look for numbers outside the house. When traveling in the car or walking around the neighborhood, find numbers. Look for numbers on the car's speedometer, clock, radio and license plates. Look on house and street signs, road signs, billboards and cash register tapes.

Step 3-More Ideas

In the grocery store, let your child call out the prices of items you place in the cart. Ask him to notice if the cashier reads the prices aloud as they are checked out. (In some stores, cashiers are required to call out the price of each item).

Look through the newspaper to circle numbers found in headlines.

Step 4-Reward

Help your child decorate the cover of a favorite book, a door or a wall in his room with numbers. They can be handmade or cut from newspapers and magazines. Numbers of all colors and sizes make colorful decorations.

Math On The Move
Counting Jumps And Jogs

This activity will give you and your child exercise. It will teach children number and measuring skills.

Learning Together

To be healthy, people need to exercise. Exercise helps children's muscles grow. Exercise helps keep adults in shape.

Jumping and jogging are easy, no-cost ways to get exercise. In this activity, the whole family exercises together.

Did You Know

Exercises use up extra calories. A calorie measures the energy giving power of foods. How many calories the body needs depend in part upon how active a person is.

Many adults get fat as they grow older. They eat the same amount of food but they become less active.

One thick slice of bread has 100 calories. If an inactive person eats a thick slice of bread every day, it can add 10 pounds a year.

Exercise "burns up" extra calories and fat.

Help To Make This Activity Work

Get your child his own measuring tape. Write his name on the tape with magic marker.

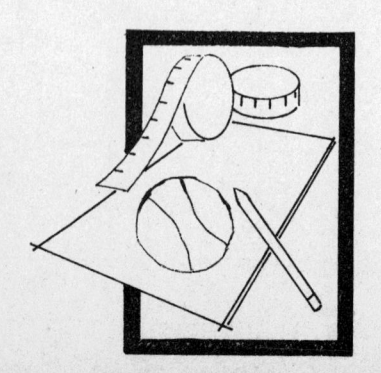

Step 1-Materials

Ball (any large, round ball that bounces)
Measuring tape
Paper
Pencil
TV, radio, or record player

Step 2-Doing It

1. Choose a place indoors that's safe for jumping and for bouncing balls. If the weather is good, choose a place outside. Turn on some music.

2. Think of this as a easy exercise plan for a few days. Each day you will do more exercise.

   <u>Day One</u>. Bounce the ball at least 5 times. Jump in place at least 5 times. Jog for at least one minute.

   Everyday you and your child can time each other. Count to be sure that each of you does your part.

   <u>Day Two</u>. Bounce the ball at least 10 times. Jump in place at least 10 times. Jog for at least two minutes.

   <u>Day Three</u>. Bounce the ball at least 15 times. Jump in place at least 15 times. Jog for at least three minutes. (You can do more. Be sure to keep track of what you both do.)

3. Have a contest. Get all members of the family to take turns doing these exercises. Who can bounce the ball the longest time?

Step 3-More Ideas

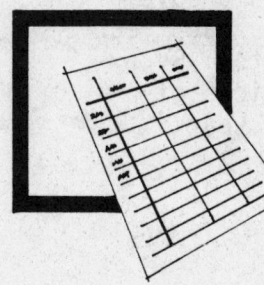

Keep track of each person's exercise totals. Mary jumped 5 times on <u>Day One</u>. How many times did she jump on <u>Day Two</u>? Try to keep this record.

Use the tape measure to measure family members' heights. Instead of a regular tape measure use a metric tape measure, if you have one.

Count the stairs as you go up or down.

Use a wrist watch with a second hand to time your running in place

Step 4-Reward

A good place to exercise is the roller skating rink. A family trip to the roller skating rink or a bowling alley would be a good reward.

Paper Bag Walk
Picking Up For Fun and Cleaning Up For Good

This activity will give children practice counting with real objects. It's fun to count and collect leaves, rocks and sticks while you walk together outdoors.

Learning Together

Counting and grouping help children with their basic math skills. They can see that the number of objects is the same as written numbers. When you're outside you can point out litter. You can talk about how to prevent littering.

Did You Know

The most well known plan to stop litter has to do with soda pop bottles and cans. Some people want a national law to put all beverages into returnable bottles. These bottles would be returned to stores for money-back deposits. Some states already have these laws. The U. S. Environmental Protection Agency found that such a program could reduce roadside container litter greatly. It would save tons of aluminum, steel and glass each year. Oil is used to make these products. By returning bottles and cans, millions of barrels of oil can be saved each year.

Help To Make This Activity Work

Show interest and talk about the "treasures" that your child collects on his walk. This shows him that you care. Help the child learn not to pick leaves off trees or other growing things and not take things such as flowers or pebbles from other people's lawns.

Step 1-Materials

Paper lunch bags or grocery bags, one for each person on the walk
Paper
Strong white glue
Nature samples: anything you both want to collect

Step 2-Doing It

1. Explain that you both will collect nature samples on a walk.

2. Go for your walk. Fill your bags.

3. Count all the nature treasures that you and your child have collected. You might look at who collected the largest and the smallest sized treasure.

4. Ask your child some questions. How many of the same kinds of objects did we collect? How many acorns or leaves from the same tree? How many 3 leaf clovers, flat or smooth stones were collected?

5. Ask if your child would like to make a gift using the nature samples. Would he like to make one for himself? Suggest a "collage." He can make a collage by pasting nature samples on a piece of paper.

6. Talk about with whom he can share this gift. It could be a neighbor or a senior citizen he knows. Good citizenship is built by doing things for others.

7. Help your child make the gift of his choice.

Step 3-More Ideas

This activity is especially good for children's clubs or group walks. Even birthday party groups enjoy these walks. You can also have some supervised neighborhood clean-up walks. Doing something useful can be fun and creative.

The weather may not be nice enough for an outdoor walk. Then you could "walk" through the house to find scrap materials and objects. Your child could make a gift from this "beautiful junk."

Step 4-Reward

Praise your child's efforts. You could put up a sign at his "work space" that says "Gift Shop." A "work space" is any place your child uses to do work or make gifts.

The Time Of Our Lives
Making A Time Chart

This activity will help the whole family become more aware of time. Adults in the home can help children learn what must be done. Keeping track of their daily routine helps children learn to organize. Knowing how to organize is necessary for school success.

Learning Together

Organization helps families do tasks that need to be done. It gives families time to do other activities. Knowing how to organize is important for both children and adults.

Did You Know

An important family task is health care. Immunization of children can prevent serious disease. It is sometimes easy to forget needed immunizations. A time chart helps a family see when they need to go to a doctor or clinic. The American Academy of Pediatrics has recommended these immunization times.

Approximate Age	Immunization
2 months; repeat at 4 months and 6 months	Diphtheria-pertussis (whooping cough)-Tetanus plus oral polio vaccine
12 months	Measles vaccine (or combined measles-mumps-rubella vaccine) Tuberculin test (and every year or 18 months thereafter)
12-24 months	Rubella vaccine; mumps vaccine (if not given in combination with measles vaccine)
18 months	Diphtheria-pertussis-tetanus booster Oral polio booster
4-6 years	Diphtheria-pertussis-tetanus booster Oral polio booster
14-16 years	Diphtheria-tetanus booster
Thereafter	Diphtheria-tetanus booster every 10 years

Help To Make This Activity Work

Be sure that the household clock that you and your child use has large numbers and is easy to read. See that it is located in a place where your child can see it easily.

Step 1-Materials

Crayon
Ruler
Pencil
Paper
Clock

Step 2-Doing It

1. Prepare a daily time chart. Put a large piece of lined paper on the refrigerator door. It can be "decorated" by your child. Place a pen or pencil nearby so that jotting down times is easy.

2. Help record your child's day by listing activities and writing down the times. Start with the earliest morning activity. Try to keep a record for 1 day.

3. Your chart might look like this:

My Day

Time	Activity
7:30 a.m.	Woke up.
8:00 a.m.	Ate breakfast.
8:30 a.m.	Started for school.

If your child can write, he can jot down his own times. Otherwise, ask him to dictate his ideas and help him read time. Pictures should also be used with children who can't read. They can draw them alone, or you can help.

4. Before bed, look at the chart with your child. Take a few minutes to talk about the day and how he spent his time. Did he enjoy what he did during the day? How long did your child spend on different activities?

Step 3-More Ideas

Notice the time on a clock. Perform a simple activity like brushing teeth. (Brushing teeth is preventive health care. Brushing teeth at least twice a day can prevent tooth disease.) Check the clock again. How many minutes did the activity take?

Together, set a timer (or watch a second hand on a clock) for one minute. Talk about what you saw, heard and did in that time. A minute can feel like a long time.

Step 4-Reward

Ask your child to copy the face of a clock onto a paper plate. Cut the clock hands out of cardboard. They can be fastened with a bobby pin or fastener. Ask your child to choose his favorite time of day. Move the clock hands to show this time.

Food And Money
"Stocking" A Store At Home

This activity will help children become aware of prices. This activity is an old one but a good one. How much do things cost? Save your empty containers. Children can learn what you paid for the item.

Learning Together

Children should learn to recognize prices of store items. When children buy things they will learn when to get change and how much.

Children will also get practice in reading math abbreviations. These abbreviations include lb. (pound) and qt. (quart). Look for metric abbreviations like g (gram).

Did You Know

Most supermarkets carry about 9,000 products. These products cost different prices. The variety is exciting. But as a shopper you need to make choices.

Children need to learn to read prices and contents very carefully.

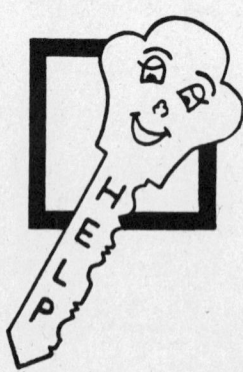

Help To Make This Activity Work

Use real cans and boxes of food from your cupboard or recently emptied boxes. Open the cans so that the stamped price and labels remain. Be sure containers are clean. Check that the cans are smooth and will not cut.

Step 1-Materials

Empty food boxes and cans with
  prices still on them
Pencil
Paper

Step 2-Doing It

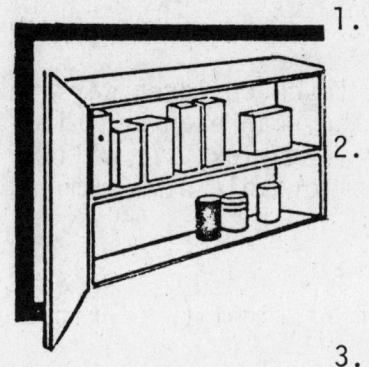

1. Save some empty cans and containers. A week's worth of cereal boxes, soup cans and laundry supplies will do. Try to save at least 10 items.

2. Together, look carefully at each container. Your child may need your help to:

    Find and read the price aloud
    Find and read any abbreviations on the outside of the cans

3. Ask him to put all cans and containers that cost 50¢ or less in one pile. (Explain that all numbers 1 to 50 will fall in this pile.) Make sure he understands.

4. Then put all cans and containers that cost from 51¢ to $1.00 in another pile.

5. Make a third pile of cans and containers that cost $1.00 or more.

6. A kindergartner or first grader will need your help to read the prices. A second and third grader may want to make a list of the prices in each pile.

7. For children who enjoy this activity, you can begin saving a new batch of cans and containers. The old ones can go into the trash or be used for "playing store."

Step 3-More Ideas

Use a grocery store receipt for this activity. Your child can use the receipt to find the item and its price. He can check the items off the list as they are put away.

The empty cartons are a good start for "playing store." Children love to buy and sell with play money. Use the play money that comes with board games.

Step 4-Reward

Go to the grocery store together. Let your child pick one special item of his choice. You can set the price limit-- let's say up to 50¢. Now he can read prices. He'll be delighted with the chance to make his choice.

Stepping Out
Hands, Feet, And Fingers Can Measure

This activity will teach children ways to measure lengths. They can even do this without a ruler or yardstick. It will help them become comfortable with numbers.

Learning Together

It's important to know how to get almost right (approximate) measurements.

Few of us carry rulers or yardsticks with us when we shop. We learn to make "working guesses" (estimations). We measure with our finger for short items. We use our feet for long items and our arm's length for even longer items. This activity shows that an object can be measured in different ways. Knowing this will help us get used to the metric system of measurement. The United States is switching to the metric system in the 1980's.

Did You Know

The words "foot," "inch" and "yard" for measurement came from olden times. The word "foot" comes from the size of a typical man's foot. A man's foot used to be only 12 inches long.

An inch was the distance from the tip of the finger to the first knuckle.

A yard was the distance from the thumb on the stretched arm to the nose or 36 inches.

A "hand" measured the width of the palm of the hand (about 4 inches). Horses are still measured in this way. A large horse is about 17 "hands" high.

Help To Make This Activity Work

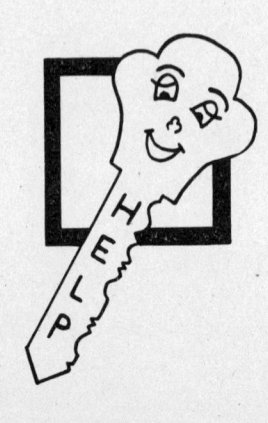

Ask your child to write down what part of his body he used as a measure for getting a certain length. For example, "My bed is 5 of my feet wide."

Step 1-Materials

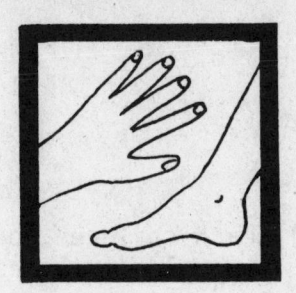

Feet, fingers, arms
Pen, pencil and paper
Objects or places to measure such as
   a room, a couch or a candle.

Step 2-Doing It

1. Talk about sizes of objects around the house. For example, the table is bigger than the chair. The rug is shorter than the length of the room.

2. Talk about what can be used to estimate these sizes when you don't have a ruler.

3. Suggest that you can use feet to estimate lengths.

4. You can put your feet (toe-to-heel) in front of one another to "walk off" the length of an object.

5. Help your child write down how long an object is. Use the toe-to-heel method. For example, the table is 7 of my feet long.

6. Take turns with your child stepping off lengths. Help him write how long an object is using your feet. For example, the wall in the living room is 10 of mother's feet wide.

7. Other family members can measure too. Your child can list and read all of these measurements.

Step 3-More Ideas

Measure something using hands. For example, how many hands tall is the vase? "The vase is 3 of my hands tall." Short items can be measured with finger lengths. One part of an adult finger is about one inch long.

Step 4-Reward

Measure your way to the nearest ice cream treat. It might be in your own refrigerator freezer, the passing ice cream truck, or the nearest drug store.

Ask your child to estimate (guess) in feet how far it is to the ice cream. Write down this estimate.

Check the estimate with facts. Walking toe to heel, measure the way. Talk about how close or far the estimate was to the real distance.

The ice cream will taste so good.

Water Magic
Learning Math From Hot And Cold

This activity will teach children to compare the effect of heat and cold on water.

Learning Together

Children should learn science and practice math at home. For example, heat and cold can change what water and food look like. Talk together about the changes you both see.

Did You Know

Everything in the world is made up of small pieces called "molecules." Heat and cold affect how tightly molecules fit together.

When water boils, molecules loosen and bounce up from the surface. They escape into the air as a gas, called steam. When water freezes, the molecules trap tiny bubbles of air between them. This is why you need to leave room as water turns to ice. Ice has bubbles in it. The bubbles take up room.

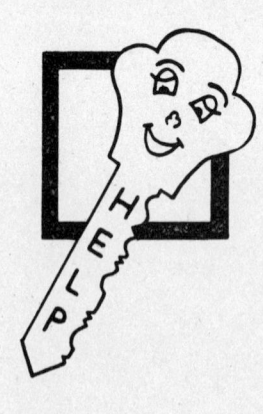

Help To Make This Activity Work

This activity could spill some water. Spread newspaper on the floor near the refrigerator, sink and stove to catch the drops. Boil water with the child. Keep the heat low. Tell your child about the need for safety at the stove.

Step 1-Materials

Ice cubes
Ice tray
Pan
Measuring Cup
Bowl
Water

Step 2-Doing It

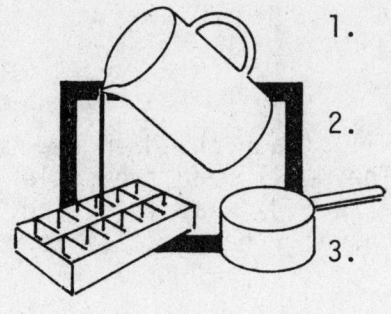

1. Ask your child these questions. What is the hottest thing in our kitchen? What is the coldest thing?

2. Use the measuring cup. Ask your child to fill the ice cube tray with water. Does it take 2 cups? 1½ cups? Show him these markings on the measuring cup.

3. Place the filled tray in the freezer. After 3 hours ask your child to see if it is frozen. If it is not, check again in 3 more hours or the next day. Ask your child whether the ice takes up more or less room in the ice tray than the water. (The ice should take up more room.)

4. Make steam! Put ½ cup of water into a saucepan on the stove. Boil the water for a few minutes. The water turns into another form when steam appears. It turns into a gas. It goes up into the air. The ice cube, the liquid water and the steam are all water. The ice cube is a solid; the water itself is a liquid; and steam is a gas.

Step 3-More Ideas

Your child might enjoy measuring cup practice at the kitchen sink. How many ¼ or ½ cups does it take to fill 1 cup? Ask a third grader how many ½ cups it takes to fill 2 cups?

A candy thermometer can be used to measure the temperature of boiling water, tap water, and ice water. Watch the mercury go up and down.

Step 4-Reward

Let your child make colored ice cubes. Put vegetable coloring in the water before it freezes.

Here's a simple frozen dessert a child can make.

"Pink Snow"

2 cups water
¼ cup of sugar
1 (3 oz.) package red jello
1½ cups imitation whipped cream

Dissolve jello and sugar in 1 cup boiling water. Add 1 cup cold water. Chill until slightly thick. Beat (with hand or electric mixer) the cream into the jello. Pour into 2 ice cube trays and freeze. Eat and enjoy!

Weigh Me
Finding Out What Scales Show

This activity will teach children how to use a scale. They will read the scale and write down (record) what they read. Grocery stores usually have scales to weigh produce.

Learning Together

Children should know how to read and to record numbers in real life situations. These include shopping in the grocery store, using the telephone and writing their address. Children work with numbers in school. But they need more chances to practice with numbers outside of school.

This activity provides a chance for children to work with fractions. They might weigh and record one-fourth (¼) of a pound or one and one-half (1½) pounds. They will learn to use the abbreviation for pound (lb.)

Did You Know

The United States measurement system will change to metrics in the 1980's. The metric system is used by most of the world. New scales in stores will have kilograms instead of pounds.

The metric system is based on units of tens. In the metric system the basic unit of weight is a gram. A gram is about the weight of a paperclip. A kilogram (1000 grams) is a little more than 2 pounds. A person who weighs 128 pounds will weigh 58 kilograms. Until we get used to the new system, it will seem as if we all have lost weight.

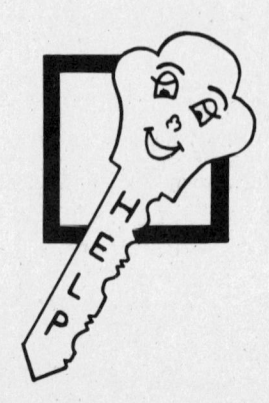

Help To Make This Activity Work

Find a scale that your child can reach and read. Then he can easily put items on the scale and read the numbers. A good place to find a scale is in the fruit and vegetable section of your supermarket. Choose a day and time when the store is not too busy.

Step 1-Materials

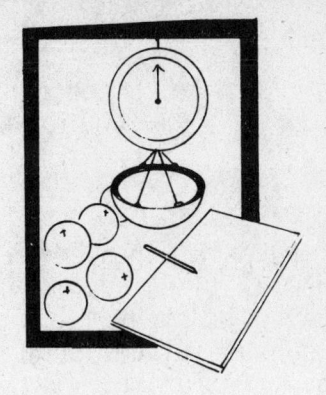

Store scale
Fruit and vegetable items to be weighed
Pencil/pen
Paper

Step 2-Doing It

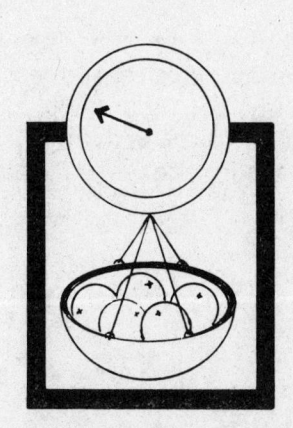

1. Look at the numbers on the scale. First find the pound (lb.) and half pound (½ lb.) marks. Then, help find the quarter (¼ lb.). Look for other fractions of a pound.

2. Choose four or five produce items to weigh. These items might be onions, potatoes, or peaches.

3. Help your child weigh each of the items separately. You will probably need to help your kindergartner and first grader read and write down the weights. Which weighs the most? Which weighs the least? You might weigh 2 lbs. of potatoes, 1 lb. of onions or ½ lb. of apples.

4. Ask your child to put two or three of the same fruits on the scale. Guess what the weight would be if one of the fruits is taken off. For example, three apples on the scale may equal (=) 1½ lbs. When you take one apple away, read the scale again. What is the weight now?

5. Praise your child's efforts and answers.

Step 3-More Ideas

Use a bathroom scale, if you have one. Your child can read and record his own weight. Other family members might want him to read and to record their weights, too.

Step 4-Reward

At the supermarket, help your child choose a piece of fruit to take home to eat. Help him weigh it, figure its cost and then pay the cashier. Fruit is good to eat. It is good for your child. He will feel proud of himself and his ability to work with scales.

Entertainments Near and Far
Figuring Distances And Time

This activity will help children begin to figure out (compute) time and distance math problems. They will start a family "fun file." They can use places they have visited or want to visit for the file.

Learning Together

Children can figure out how far away a place is that they like. How long does it take to get there? Even young children can learn to compute time and distance. They can count up the hours or minutes on a real clock. You can help them add up distances (miles) on the car's mileage meter (the odometer). This is good practice in math.

Did You Know

Much is said about Americans' traveling a lot. But over 66% of the nation's population never travels more than 100 miles from home. We stay close to home, but we drive a lot around our communities. We drive over 300 billion (one billion = one thousand million) miles a year.

Americans spend about 6% of all total yearly income on recreation. This is about $40 billion dollars a year.

Help To Make This Activity Work

Together, think of amusements that are close to home. Remember the ice cream store or the park. Use places that are no farther than 10 miles or one-half hour away. This will keep the figuring simple.

If you don't remember the exact mileage or time, don't hesitate to make guesses. Time the trip with a clock. Look at the numbers on the car mileage meter. Were your guesses close?

Step 1-Materials

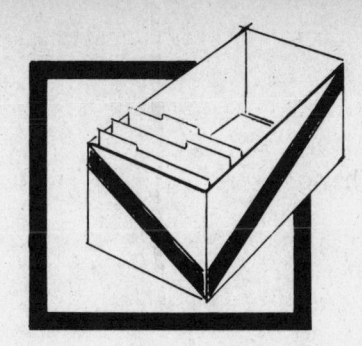

Paper (three or four pieces cut to the size of the
    file or shoe box)
Pencil, pen or crayon
A shoe box or file box
Scissors

Step 2-Doing It

1. Talk with your child about the fun places the family has visited.

2. Help decide which places the family enjoyed the most.

3. Help write information about each favorite place on separate pieces of paper. This may be a good way:

   > The Place Name_____
   > How Far From Home (miles)?_____
   > How Long To Get There (time)?_____
   > Cost (admissions, etc.)_____
   > Why My Family Liked This Place_____

4. Ask the rest of the family to add their ideas on the other side of the paper. For example, "This state park really has a good swimming pool." "This bowling alley has special times for families to bowl together."

5. Set up the file box to store this information for the family. Decorate the box.

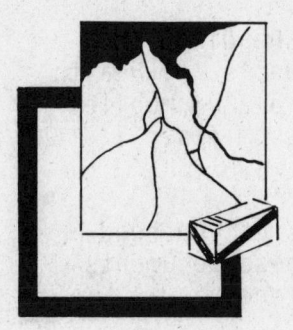

Step 3-More Ideas

1. Post a local map. Set the file box near it. Mark the map with a star (*) for every place that is put in the file box.

2. Attach a post card or snapshot of the amusement place to the file cards. Put them in your "fun file."

Step 4-Reward

The family can think of a trip to a new place. If your child likes to draw, he can make a sketch of the place. Add this to the family entertainment.

My Very Own Place
Making A Place At Home For School Things

This activity will teach children to make a school box. They will practice using a ruler for measuring and decorating the box.

Learning Together

When children are involved in organizing their school materials, they are taking a step toward success in school. You should not have to remind them to take their pencils or books to school. Encourage them to be responsible. Help them make a box for their materials. Writing out a list of daily jobs and appointments helps adults to organize each day. At the end of the day, the list reminds us of all that we have been able to do. It helps us plan for the next day.

Did You Know

Every family needs to keep its own records. This saves time and money. A good way is to put papers in a metal file box that won't burn. You can use large manila envelopes to store the papers inside the file box.

Here is a handy list for envelope headings:
1) House 2) Life insurance 3) Debts 4) Health insurance 5) Personal documents 6) Automobile 7) Taxes 8) Bank records 9) Investments 10) Employee benefits 11) Wills.

Records are always useful. Sometimes you need family information in a hurry. These documents are really needed in case of emergency.

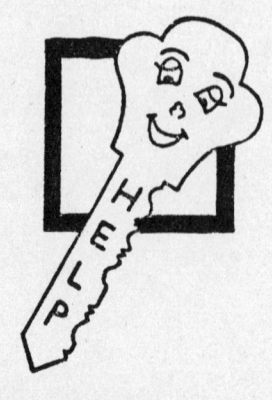

Help To Make This Activity Work

Your child will be proud of the materials box because you made it together. You can encourage good habits. Praise your child's use of the box for his school books and materials. Be sure to place the box close to the door. Then it will be easy to get into the habit of using it.

Step 1-Materials

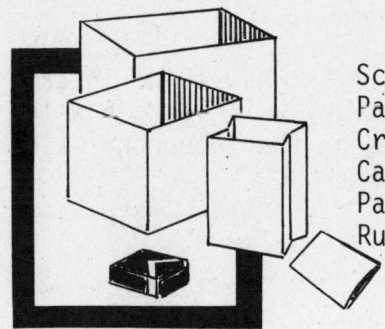

Scissors
Paste, glue or tape
Crayons or magic markers
Cardboard box (about the size of a shoe or boot box)
Paper for covering the box--grocery store bags will do
Ruler

Step 2-Doing It

1. Talk about the things needed for school. Your child may need a pencil, his lunch, or something to share with friends. He may need his homework or a library book. Discuss the idea of making a handy school box to keep near the door. He can put all of his school things in the box in the evening. Then they will not be forgotten in the morning.

2. Find the box and the wrapping to be used to cover it.

3. Use a ruler to measure each side of the box. Cut a section of the wrapping paper to fit each side. Paste or tape the paper to the sides of the box.

4. Ask your child to make colorful designs. Have him write his name on the box. He can use crayons or magic markers.

5. Help him to find a good place to put the box.

Step 3-More Ideas

Encourage and help your child to make boxes for other things around the house. For example, one box might be made to hold screws, nuts, bolts, nails and small tools. Another would be handy for "cents off" store coupons. Children's shoe boxes are perfect for these smaller items.

Step 4-Reward

Write a short, easy-to-read note to your child. He can read it himself, or you can read it to him. Let the whole family sign it. For example, it might say, "We like the school box you made. It has pretty pictures on it and helps to keep your school things neat. Love..."

As a reward for using the box regularly, leave special mystery messages in the box for your child.

SOS
Learning To Handle Emergencies

Children will learn what to do in case of emergency. They will learn how to get help, by using the telephone or by asking a neighbor.

Learning Together

Children should learn how to call for help. They should know how to identify themselves and to tell where they are located. Emergency telephone numbers are rarely used. However, children and even adults should know what number to call if necessary. Practice dialing emergency numbers with children. Practice how to call on neighbors for help. Then they will be prepared if there is a real emergency.

Did You Know

Emergency numbers are listed at the beginning of a telephone book. Fire, Police and Poison Control numbers are listed. Suppose you need emergency help but do not have a telephone book. You can dial "O" for operator anywhere in the United States. The operator who answers will tell you the number you need or call it for you.

When you call for emergency help you should give the exact location where help is needed. You must also give your name and the telephone number from which you are calling.

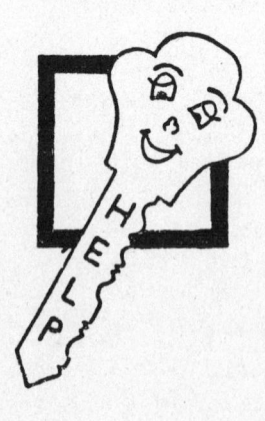

Help To Make This Activity Work

1. Ask a neighbor, friend or relative to help out in an emergency. Practice asking this person for help.

2. Practice makes perfect. Practice dialing. Use a child's toy telephone. You may also hold down the button of the receiver while he uses a real telephone. You can pretend to be the person on the other end of the line.

Step 1-Materials

Toy or real telephone
A local telephone directory
Pen/pencil
Paper
Tape

Step 2-Doing It

1. Discuss several kinds of emergencies with your child. Talk about why it is useful to know the numbers to call in case of an emergency.

2. Together, look in the telephone book for the listing of the numbers. Examples include the fire department, the police and the local hospital. If your child can't read, make a picture chart with the numbers. Put a picture of a fire next to the fire department number.

3. Talk about which family member, neighbor or friend he should contact in an emergency. Don't forget to put this person's name on the picture chart.

4. If your child can read and write, help him list all emergency numbers on a sheet of paper.

Name	Number
Aunt Sue	372-2110

5. Show him how to read and dial these numbers. Let him practice dialing by himself (with a toy telephone). Take turns playing a game of pretend. First, he can dial the emergency number and you can answer the call. Then you dial the emergency number and he can answer the call.

6. Teach him to tell his name and address slowly and clearly to the person to whom he's talking.

7. Post the emergency number list or picture chart at your child's eye level. Put it close to your telephone.

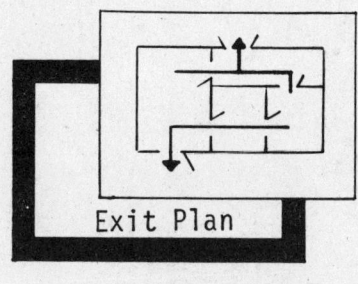

Step 3-More Ideas

To prepare for fire emergencies, walk through the house. Point out possible exits. Explain the safe way to exit. Decide on a safe place for the family to meet outside the house. Have some practice fire drills.

Step 4-Reward

Visit the local fire or police department. Let your child look at the equipment. Let him talk to the firefighters and policemen. Ask him to share his new emergency number knowledge with the firefighters or policemen. Ask them to explain how they receive and respond to calls.

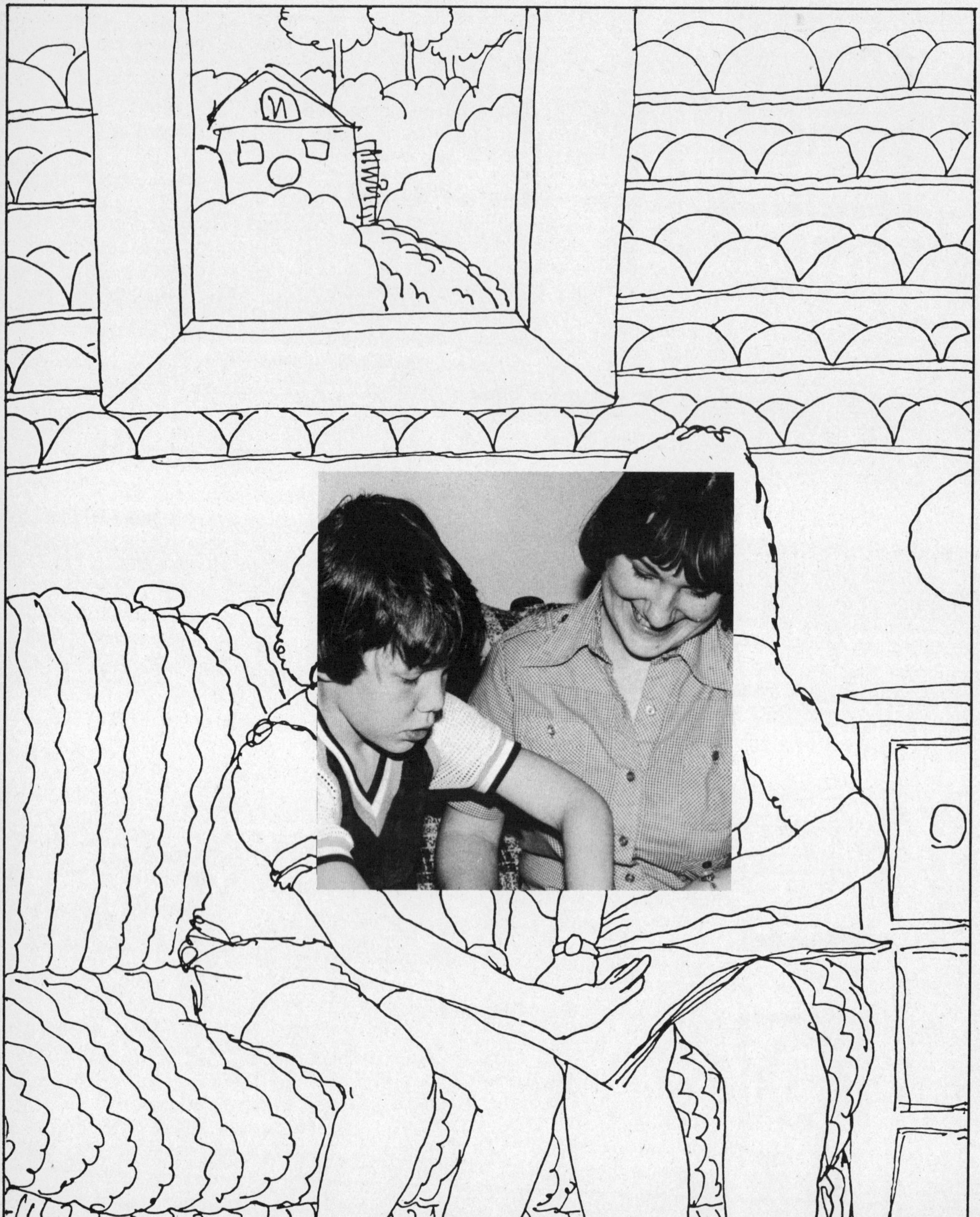

READING: GRADES FOUR TO SIX

The 12 home learning "recipes" in this section are arranged for the children from easiest to hardest.

The listing below gives a special learning for the adults and a special learning for the children in each "recipe."

1. **Objects Tell Occupations**
   Adults learn that children need to start to think about their future jobs at an early age.
   Children learn about the many people and skills needed in different jobs.

2. **Visiting Older People**
   Adults learn about the needs of today's new group of older people.
   Children learn how to use their own skills to make an older person happy.

3. **Business Walk**
   Adults learn how to find needed information about local community business services.
   Children learn about many kinds of local businesses offering goods and services to their family.

4. **Family Directory**
   Adults learn how to help children keep in touch with relatives and friends.
   Children learn to use the alphabet to locate names.

5. **How Much Is It?**
   Adults learn to use catalogs and newspapers to find the most economical places to shop.
   Children learn how important it is to read and to compare prices before buying.

6. **Fill In The Blanks**
   Adults learn about the costs of buying on credit.
   Children learn through practice to read and to fill out forms carefully.

7. **Personal Health File**
   Adults learn about the importance of keeping health records for all family members.
   Children learn to chart their own health record. The health record includes immunizations, height and weight changes and childhood diseases.

8. **Button, Button**
   Adults learn that many men and women are interested in fixing and styling their own clothes.
   Children learn to take responsibility for the care of their own clothes.

9. **What Do You Think?**
   Adults learn that there are different ways of listening. Some ways work better than others to help people express themselves.
   Children learn to listen and to understand different opinions.

10. **Operation Alert**
    Adults learn about household products that injure children if they are swallowed or handled.
    Children learn how to recognize dangerous products by reading their labels.

11. **Child Care By The Hour**
    Adults learn to teach basic child care for babysitting.
    Children learn how to take care of a younger child safely.

12. **Who's In The News?**
    Adults learn about ways to encourage their children to want to know about current events.
    Children learn to use daily news to find out more about how governments work.

Objects Tell Occupations
Using Household Objects To Learn About Jobs

This activity, which is like a game, will help children learn about jobs. Objects in your own home are made by people at work. A table, a lamp or a book are good "take-off" points for conversations about jobs.

Learning Together

Children should start to think about the world of work. They can learn about different jobs from objects found at home. A glass is made somewhere by people and machines. So is a chair and so is a pot. Talk about the differences between handmade and manufactured items. Talk about new products today that did not exist when you were a child.

Did You Know

It's a good idea for adults also to think about different jobs. Every year jobs disappear and new ones replace them. Computer jobs have only existed for a few years.

Half of the people now working hold different jobs from the ones for which they were trained. Today people are changing jobs more often. People often hold more than one job.

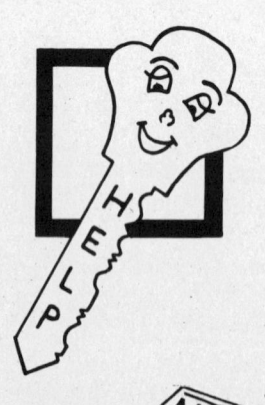

Help To Make This Activity Work

Ask your child to think about the jobs people in the family do. Make a list of these. Think about jobs no one in the family has done but might be able to do.

Adult help may be needed: You might say to your child, "Do you remember Uncle Joe who was a milkman and Aunt Liz who was a supermarket checker?"

Step 1-Materials

Any three objects in the home
    For example, a newspaper, the radio or a house plant.

Step 2-Doing It

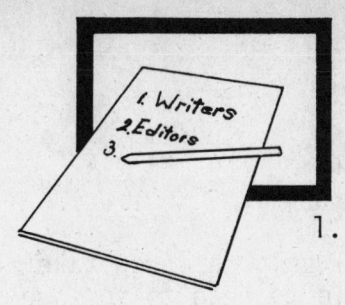

1. Let your child choose 3 objects in your home to talk about.

2. Ask him to think of all the jobs needed to make these objects. The family can join in to talk about these jobs.

    To make a newspaper, it takes lumberjacks, paper makers, ink makers, printers, writers, and so on.

    To get plants into your house it takes growers, truck drivers, and florists.

Step 3-More Ideas

Try the same activity with three more articles. You might try a pencil, a toothbrush, and the telephone.

Plan a family trip to visit a place where people work. Visit a factory, a dairy or a hospital.

Step 4-Reward

Ask your child to surprise the family with a "mystery" object for a dinner table game. It can be new, used or borrowed. It might be a library book, a brick, a paper bag.

Talk about: "What is it made of? Where does it come from? What kinds of jobs helped to make it?" Keep track of who lists the most jobs.

Visiting Older People
Brightening The Days For The Elderly

This activity will help children take pride in being able to read to someone in the community. They will do something to make another person happy.

Learning Together

It is important for children to learn to reach out to others. Our society depends on the help that people give to one another. Children in the upper elementary grades may like community service. It can give them good feelings and a sense of purpose.

Did You Know

There were twice as many Americans alive in 1975 as in 1920. In 1920, the average life span was 54 years. In 1975 it was 72 years. People live longer now because of better nutrition and medical care. Often these later years are retirement years. Older citizens may be lonely because they no longer work. They may live far away from family and friends.

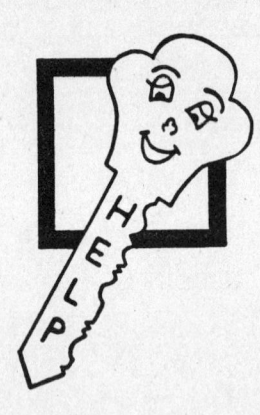

Help To Make This Activity Work

Do you know an elderly person to whom your child can read? Is there an older relative he would like to visit? A local social service agency will have names of older shut-ins in your area. If you belong to a religious group, ask your pastor, priest or rabbi.

You may want to ask if the older person has any special reading interests. Your child should be able to read the material well. To do this, he may have to practice at home. Before beginning, talk about how long your child should read. Ten to fifteen minutes may be a good length of time. Talk about this before your child reads so that no one will be disappointed.

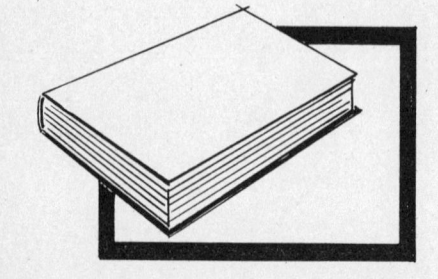

Step 1-Materials

A book or magazine

Step 2-Doing It

1. Contact the person to whom your child will be reading to make a date for a first visit. Introduce yourselves.

2. Let your child tell a little about himself and his family. Let him listen to his new friend tell about himself.

3. Say that your child would like to read to him for 10 or 15 minutes. Before you go, talk with your child about reading materials that you could bring.

4. Suggest that your child read only a short time the first day.

5. Later at home, practice the reading selected for the second visit.

6. Visit your older friend again and read as planned.

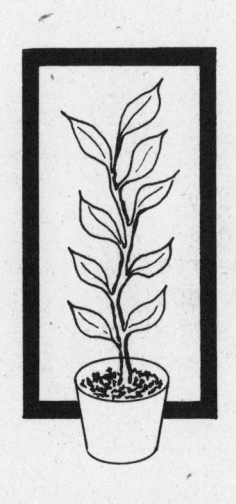

Step 3-More Ideas

You might both like to go back a third time. He can take a little gift to his "special friend." He might take a few homemade cookies, a plant, or a story he's written. Ask him to share stories of things that happened at school.

Ask the "special friend" about his childhood. This is a good way to understand history and past events. Your child will learn about different times and places.

Write notes or cards to the "special friend" in between visits. Older people like to receive notes. This gives your child practice in letter writing.

Step 4-Reward

Helping others can give children a special feeling. This activity may count as a service project for Girl Scouts, Boy Scouts, Cub Scouts, Brownie or Campfire Girls. By helping others, children will help themselves. They will realize that not all happiness comes from things, like toys or clothes. Some of the best things in life really are free.

Business Walk
Learning About Your Neighborhood

This activity will help children learn about the shops and businesses in their community. They can learn how to find services in the telephone book. They can look in the yellow pages to find what shops are in the community.

Learning Together

Children should know their business community. They will be better shoppers if they know where to go for what they need. The next time you need a business service, ask which one your young shopper would like to use. Help him use the telephone book to find the address and telephone number.

Try the business that he suggests. If you can't, give him the reason why you can't. For example, it might be too expensive. You might not like the product. It might be too far away.

Did You Know

You can check on a product before you buy it. Read consumer magazines at your local library. You can call your local or nearest Better Business Bureau for information about the store you plan to use. If there is no Better Business Bureau, you can call the local Chamber of Commerce.

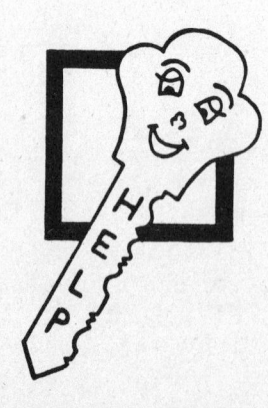

Help To Make This Activity Work

Ask your child which business or store in your community he would like to visit. Let him pick a local neighborhood business from the yellow pages.

Step 1-Materials

Stores and businesses in your community
For example, you might visit a grocery store, meat market, dairy, bakery or garage.

Step 2-Doing It

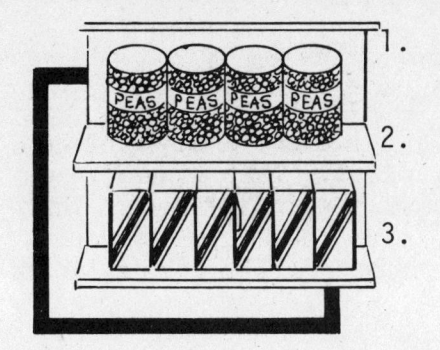

1. Walk or ride to the business. Stop outside the store to look at the window displays.

2. Read the signs and advertisements. Ask your child what service he thinks the store offers.

3. Go inside the store. See how items are on the shelves and in the display cases. Ask which kinds of items are together. Ask why he thinks these products are grouped in certain ways.

4. Read the signs and posters. If possible, take some flyers home to read later.

5. Talk to the storekeeper. Ask him to tell you about his store. How is the store arranged and why? Ask him about other services he offers. Encourage your child to ask any questions he may have.

6. Have the child thank the storekeeper for his help and extra time.

7. Talk about your trip. What did your child enjoy most and why? What did your child enjoy least? Did you collect materials from the store? Be sure to read them together when you get home.

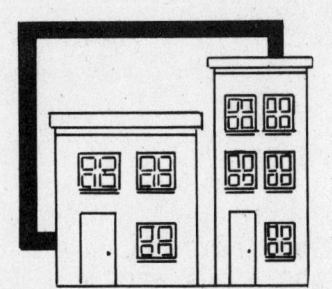

Step 3-More Ideas

Talk about the services that are offered to your community. Are there too many stores of one kind? Are there enough stores of another kind? Do you need to go out of your community for most of the services you need?

Encourage your child to think about what must be done to open a new business of his own. What special training would he need? What services would he offer? Does he think his business would make money?

Step 4-Reward

Arrange a trip to see what happens in a business "behind the scenes." You could watch a baker make donuts. You could see a shoemaker repair shoes or a butcher cut meats.

Family Directory
Making An Alphabetical List of Family Names

This activity will give children practice in alphabetizing names. They will make a list of names of family and friends. These names will be put in alphabetical order. Their telephone numbers will also be listed.

Learning Together

Words can be alphabetized using the first letter. But words must also be alphabetized by the second, third or fourth letters. Smith, Smyth, Somes and Swans are listed alphabetically. They are listed according to their second and third letters.

Did You Know

People are using the telephone more than ever these days. It's helpful for children to know how to get in touch with their families. Many family members now live far apart. The telephone has become an important way to keep in touch. Over 95% of all American households have a telephone. It's surprising but long distance calls cost less today than 20 years ago.

Help To Make This Activity Work

Before your child begins, have him find your name and number in the telephone directory. Note that last names are in alphabetical order. You may not have a telephone or your name may not be listed in the telephone directory. If so, help your child find the name of a friend, a neighbor, or a relative.

Step 1-Materials

Plain white paper (to be stapled together for the family list)
Scrap paper (the back of old envelopes or paper used on only one side)
Pencil/pen
Telephone directory (optional)

Step 2-Doing It

1. Ask your child to think of as many names of family members as he can. Remember aunts, uncles, cousins, friends, etc.

2. Use scrap paper to list the names of these people. Names are easier to alphabetize if all names beginning with the same letter are listed together.

3. Help alphabetize this list. Place the last name first. Double check this sheet. Be sure that all of the names are included. Then enter the names and numbers into a Family Directory. (This is the stapled paper.)

4. Ask your child to read these again. Check them against the notes to avoid errors.

5. Now you can both add the telephone numbers beside the names.

Step 3-More Ideas

This directory can be decorated with pictures your child has made. He can cut pictures from old magazines that show families doing things together.

Step 4-Reward

Put the family directory in a handy place. Family members will benefit from this activity each time the directory is used.

How Much Is It?
Reading Classified Ads To Compare Prices

This activity will help children read to get information. Children will learn that they can pay very different prices for the same product. They will learn to shop for an item they want.

Learning Together

Children should learn how to compare prices. They can practice shopping for bicycles, furniture, TV's or any item. Usable, secondhand items like these are often advertised in the classified ads. Is your family planning to buy a new product? They can check the classified ads to see how much used items cost. They can do this for a few days to see how prices vary with different ads. This is good math and reading experience.

Did You Know

Here are some tips to remember if you place a classified ad.

1. Check the costs of an ad in different newspapers. Sometimes neighborhood weeklies run "give-away" ads for free.

2. Learn about the abbreviations you can use. This will save space and money.

3. Newspapers have categories in which your ad will be placed. Your ad for a desk might go into office or into household furniture. You usually have a choice. Ask the salesperson taking your ad where it will sell best.

4. Do you want an ad to run on a certain day? Ask the newspaper office when your ad must be placed.

Help To Make This Activity Work

Together, look to see how items for sale are listed. They are in ABC order in an index at the beginning of the classified ads. Some newspapers use abbreviations to save space. If you do not understand the abbreviations, call the classified section of your newspaper.

The best buy is not always the cheapest item. Always think about the extra features each item has for the price.

Step 1-Materials

Classified ad section of the newspaper.
Pencil, crayon, or marker
Paper

Step 2-Doing It

1. Ask your child to select an item he would like to "buy" from a newspaper ad. This might be a bicycle, television set or a motorcycle.

2. Help him find the section where his item is listed.

3. Together, mark the ads that sound like the "best buys" with a crayon.

4. Ask what item he has chosen and why. Discuss with other members of the family their opinions on the ad. What do they consider to be the best buy?

Step 3-More Ideas

Try this activity with newspaper and magazine ads for <u>new</u> products. Compare classified prices on really large items such as houses or cars. This will help children begin to think about big sums of money.

Together you can write an ad that could be used in the newspaper to sell an item from your own home that you no longer need. Use abbreviations to save money. The ad must be clear. Then people will buy the item you are selling.

Step 4-Reward

Go to an auction that is advertised. Visit some garage sales that have been in the newspaper. These are fun. The prices of items provide math practice. You don't even have to buy anything!

Fill In The Blanks
Filling Out Forms And Applications

This activity will teach children to read and fill out application forms. These may be social security forms, library cards or credit card applications. They may also be job application forms.

Learning Together

Children should learn to read the fine print carefully when filling out forms. They need to learn that facts may be hidden in the fine print. For example, a book or record club may cost more than you think. Extra costs may be explained in the fine print.

Knowing how to fill out forms can help your children and your family. This is needed when you're buying something on credit. It is needed when you're applying for a job.

Did You Know

Many families do not know how much extra they pay when they buy something on the installment plan.

The cost of credit varies. You should shop around for the best deal.

Frequently credit cards charge extra fees per year on your unpaid bills. You can and should ask the dealer how much you are paying for credit. The business is required to let you know.

The Truth in Lending Law requires sales people to give you the total cost of credit. They should tell you interest, service, and carrying charges. They should also tell you about charges for required insurance.

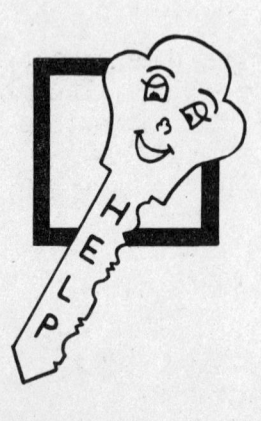

Help To Make This Activity Work

Have your child read aloud to you all of the information and questions on the application. Help him with questions and words he does not understand. Work on one section at a time. Stop if the child gets tired or bored. Continue at another time.

Step 1-Materials

Application forms: available from department
    stores, government offices, libraries, businesses
Coupons from magazines for ordering items by mail
Pen or pencil

Step 2-Doing It

1. Let your child pick out two or three forms to work on. Help him complete the information on the forms. Ask him to print neatly. Information on forms must be printed or typed. Remember that the signature line needs your child's name. That makes the form official.

2. Explain that when you sign a contract you have to live up to what is in the contract. So it is important to read and understand the fine print before signing anything.

Step 3-More Ideas

Fill out an application for a social security card together. Fill out mail-order coupons found in magazines and newspapers. Fill out school forms sent home.

Step 4-Reward

Allow your child to order a free or low-cost item from a magazine or newspaper coupon. Your child may want to order something for you!

Personal Health File
Organizing Information

Children can learn to put together their own health information. They can copy it without mistakes. They can keep this information in one place. This will teach them to be organized.

Learning Together

Children should have information about their own health history and care. This information includes their history of childhood diseases and shots (immunizations). Many families do not have this important information in one place. It is a good idea to keep all of this information together. You will need it in an emergency. Usually, you receive some records from your doctor following physical examinations. If you don't have these records, ask your doctor for them.

Did You Know

It's useful for adults to have the facts on their own personal medical history. It's especially helpful when visiting a new doctor.

Sometimes it is difficult for patients to see their own medical records. The records of your tests and X-rays are important to you. A guide to help you get this information is available from The Health Research Group, 2000 P Street, N.W., Washington, D.C. 20036.

Help To Make This Activity Work

Gather together your children's health information and records. Health records may include clinic visits, immunization dates, physical, dental and eye reports. Height and weight information are also part of the health file.

Step 1-Materials

A sturdy notebook or pieces of paper stapled together
Pen/pencil
Ruler

Step 2-Doing It

1. Read and talk about your children's health records with them. Explain the reason for each immunization.

2. Compare the changes in their weight and height as they have grown older. This will help them understand the pattern of growth.

3. Talk about the various childhood diseases they have had. Tell them how each disease made them look or feel. You might say, "With mumps, your neck and throat were swollen and painful."

4. Help your children begin a health history notebook. Have them write their name on the front of it.

5. Have your children make a chart about themselves. Guide them in using the ruler to make a table with two columns. Begin with earliest recorded information. Help them fill in the columns like this:

Age	What Happened
At birth	Weight 6 lbs. 4 ozs.
3 to 6 months	First DPT series (Diphtheria, Pertussis, Tetanus) plus oral polio vaccine
Age 2	Went to the hospital to have stitches due to a fall
Age 5	DPT booster, oral polio booster

6. Encourage them to read each item after it is copied. Each entry should be in proper time order.

Step 3-More Ideas

1. Other family members might want to include their health histories in the notebook. Then, information on family members would be recorded together. This would then be a family "reference" book.

2. When it is time for your children's next physical examination, help them look up the doctor's telephone number and make their own appointments. During the appointment ask the doctor to show how he records and keeps health information.

Step 4-Reward

Reward your children for getting organized. Give them some supplies they can use for school work. You can give them a ruler, paper clips, scissors, scotch tape, or even a stapler.

Button, Button
Fixing Clothes: Even A Child Can Do It

This activity will teach children to take care of themselves. It will improve children's hand and eye coordination.

Learning Together

Children should become well coordinated. Good coordination helps children write better. In writing, you use your hands and your eyes together.

Good coordination also helps children do better in sports, dance, crafts, and other activities.

Did You Know

Ready-made clothing takes a lot of the family budget. Many people are making clothes for themselves and their families. Women and girls are not the only ones who like to sew. At least one fourth of the boys in some high schools are taking cooking and sewing classes. Ten years ago only one tenth of the boys were taking these classes.

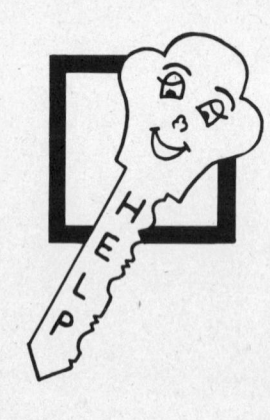

Help To Make This Activity Work

Show your child how to use the needle safely. Encourage him to keep going even if his first stitches are large and uneven.

If this is his first sewing job, help him practice on some old play clothes or scraps of cloth.

A bright patch on his blue jeans is easy and fun! Boys, as well as girls, can enjoy sewing.

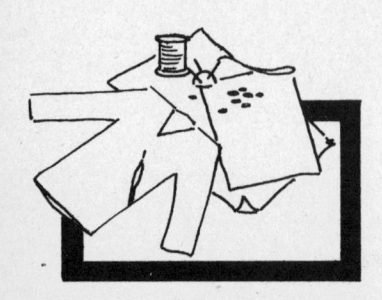

Step 1-Materials

Clothes that need buttons or easy repairs
Buttons
Needle and thread
Colorful fabric scraps

Step 2-Doing It

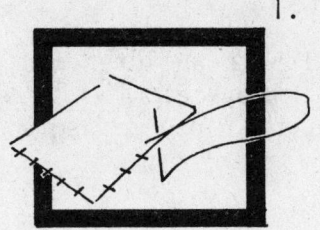

1. Help your child pick out an item that needs easy repair. Choose a button to be replaced, or a hole to be covered with a "crazy" or matching patch.

    A child will feel more important doing a real job (on play clothes) than on scraps of material.

2. Help him select the tools needed, For example, a button, the right color thread, and a needle.

3. Show your child how to thread a needle. Show him how to sew on a button or to sew on a patch. Have him watch you, step by step.

4. Now let him do a repair job on his own. Don't expect it to be perfect. Remember that children need practice to do a good job sewing.

    Replacing buttons and mending holes are necessary skills everyone should know.

Step 3-More Ideas

Your child can sew colorful scraps together to make pot holders or placemats. He can make book covers or even a quilt. Odd-shaped or colorful buttons can be sewn on for decoration.

An older child can be taught to use the sewing machine. Then, with your help he can practice sewing some fabrics together by machine.

Step 4-Reward

Point out to everyone the sewing your child has done. Encourage your child to give sewing work as gifts. These are personal gifts that are much appreciated, and they cost only a few pennies.

What Do You Think?
Taking A Home Opinion Poll

This activity will help children listen. They will learn to describe their family's feelings about products bought for home use.

Learning Together

Children can build listening skills by collecting people's opinions. They should understand the reasons for these opinions. They can learn that different people can have different points of view.

Did You Know

Listening is a skill that can be learned. There are four basic listening patterns. All can be useful in family life.

1. There is passive listening. This means being quiet while the other person talks.

2. There is attentive listening. This means nodding, or smiling and looking directly at the speaker. It shows interest and attention.

3. There is inviting others to talk by saying "I'm interested." "Would you like to talk about it?" "It sounds as if you have strong feelings about that."

4. There is active listening. In this case, you let the person know that you heard what he said. You might say, "Did I understand you to say..." Then you repeat what you think the person said. Active listening can help others express their feelings. It can promote feelings of caring and warmth between people who are talking.

Help To Make This Activity Work

When listening to people it is important not to criticize right away. If you criticize, you can put people on the defensive. Then they become angry or afraid to talk with you. Good communication means people expressing their ideas. It also means listening to each other. Then each person can find common areas of interest.

Step 1-Materials

Something the family buys that everyone in the
    house uses. It could be anything from soap
    to soup.
Pencil
Paper

Step 2-Doing It

1. Ask your child to take a poll on a product the family is using. He can ask "Should we buy more of this? If yes, why? If no, why not? What could the family buy instead of this product?"

2. Write down each family member's opinion about the product. Help him take notes on why people like or dislike the product. To do this the child must be a good listener.

3. When everyone is polled, ask your child what he has learned. Does the family like the product?

4. Talk about the results at the dinner table. They can also be shared in written form.

5. On the next shopping trip, you might buy some of the products the family suggested. The family can see its wishes come true.

Step 3-More Ideas

Your child can use the same poll with neighbors or friends. He should be encouraged to write down their comments. Make sure that your child polls neighbors who like children.

Step 4-Reward

Let him use his own opinion to choose his favorite dessert for the family.

Operation Alert
Reading Warning Labels On Products

This activity will help children read and understand the warning labels on medicines and household cleaners in the home.

Learning Together

Children should learn to read labels. If a product is dangerous, the label should warn us. Reading labels carefully may save a child's life. Children may not be able to read all the technical words. But they do need to recognize the warning words.

Did You Know

Twice as many children die accidentally from swallowing medicines as from swallowing household cleaners. It is dangerous to take medicine not prescribed by a doctor. This needs to be made clear to children.

There are almost 600 poison control centers in the United States. At these centers, information is available on how to treat people who have swallowed dangerous household products or medicines. Ask your doctor, the health clinic or call your hospital for the poison control number in your community. Keep it posted in your home.

Help To Make This Activity Work

Before starting this activity look around the house to find 4 or 5 products and medicines with warning labels. Put these in a sturdy box.

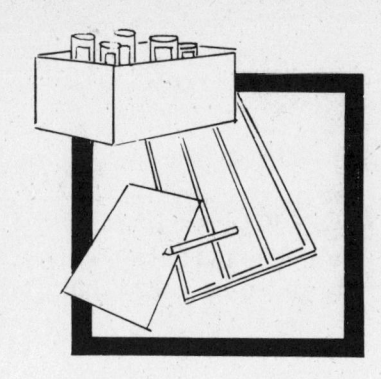

Step 1-Materials

Flat surface (table or floor)
Paper
Pen/pencil
Old newspapers
Sturdy box with 4 or 5 household products and
    medicines. Use only those with warning labels.

Step 2-Doing It

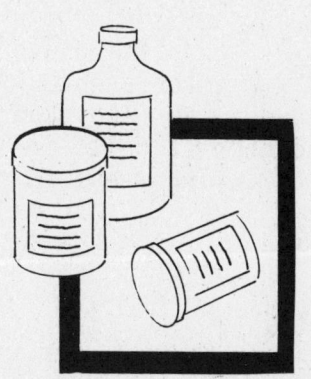

1. Spread newspaper on the flat surface.

2. Take one product out of the box. Help your child read the warning label aloud.

3. Ask him to point to the words that mean WATCH OUT. Some of these are <u>caution</u>, <u>poison</u>, <u>danger</u>, <u>warning</u>, <u>hazard</u>. Point out the skull and crossbones symbol.

4. Ask him to read the labels of the other products or medicines in the box. Help him write some of the warning words.

5. Talk about why these cleaning products and medicines are kept out of everyone's reach. Ask why they have special tops and caps.

6. Talk about what can be done if these products or medicines are swallowed accidentally. The labels tell us what remedies we can give to work against the poison. These are called "antidotes."

Step 3-More Ideas

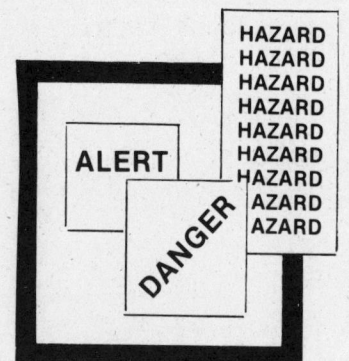

Ask your child, when he's outside, to find signs that say <u>hazard</u>, <u>caution</u>, <u>alert</u>, <u>careful</u>, <u>danger</u>, <u>watch out</u>. Look for these signs as you're driving. Where are they found? Talk about why these signs are needed.

Step 4-Reward

Put your child's list of warning words in a special place for the family to read. The refrigerator door is a very good place.

Praise him for his help in bringing these warning words to the family's attention. He has 2 rewards. He knows more about his environment. He shared with his family what he has learned.

Child Care By The Hour
Fun And Learning While Babysitting

This activity will help children practice reading skills. They will use what they have learned in school when babysitting with younger children. They will improve their babysitting skills.

Learning Together

Parents should feel secure when they allow older children to care for younger children. A practice session such as this activity will help. Children often start babysitting alone around 13 years of age. Talking about how to be a good babysitter helps children's babysitting skills. They can practice with a brother, sister or a neighbor's child in your home as a "good deed." Stay nearby during these practice sessions.

Did You Know

People need more babysitters today. More mothers have jobs outside the home during the day.

Nearly 40% of mothers with children under 5 are working outside of the home. Nearly 50% of all women with children 6 to 13 years of age are working. These are the figures as we enter the 1980's.

The Census Bureau says that almost two million children ages 7 to 13 are "latch-key" children. These are children who carry their own house keys. They have no one to care for them right after school.

This need for child care might offer jobs to women who want to stay at home.

Help To Make This Activity Work

Talk about ways to handle emergencies. Explain how to find telephone numbers for fire and police. Post them by the telephone. Post a friend's or relative's number whom your child can call for help, if you go out. Always leave a number where you can be reached.

Share your ideas on discipline with your child. Explain that a busy happy youngster won't need a lot of discipline. Plan what your child can do while babysitting. He can play a game with or read to the youngster. Instead of watching TV, he might use the time teaching the youngster his favorite games.

Step 1-Materials

Paper
Pencil

Step 2-Doing It

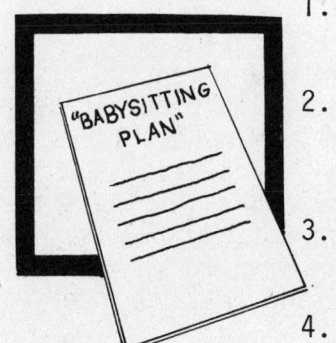

1. Ask your child to select a younger child to "adopt" for a half-hour.

2. Choose 2 stories that your child can read. Together, think of some questions about the stories to talk about with the younger child.

3. Have your child write down what he plans to do while babysitting.

4. Let your child share his experience with you after the half-hour is over.

Step 3-More Ideas

Occasionally, your child may need a sitter. He can pick a more difficult book for the sitter to read to him.

Is your child interested in babysitting? Tell your neighbors and family friends.

Step 4-Reward

Take your child to the store to pick out a special address and appointment book. He'll use this little book to keep track of his babysitting jobs. He can write in the book who wants him and the date he is wanted. Keeping an appointment book is fun. It helps to develop children's organizing abilities.

Another way to record babysitting jobs is to keep a chart. The chart might look like this:

Date	Time	Family Name	Children's Names	What We Did
Jan. 1	7:00	Smith	Paul and Mary	Played Scrabble

Who's In The News?
Keeping Up With Government

This activity will give children practice reading the daily news. The excitement of political campaigns will help them understand adult level reading.

Learning Together

Talking about people and problems in government builds your children's interest in current events. This makes them want to read about candidates in the news. Many elections come up during the year. There are city, county, state and national elections. Candidates have debates. These are written up in the newspapers. Knowing these facts will also help you teach your child about American government. It will help you choose people for office who understand what you need.

Did You Know

There are 100 United States Senators, two for each state. Senators are elected for six year terms. There are 435 members of the United States House of Representatives. They are elected for two year terms.

The number of each state's representatives depends on the state's population. States with more people have more representatives. For example, Michigan has 19 representatives. Alaska, Delaware, Nevada, North Dakota, Vermont and Wyoming each have only one representative. With each national census, these numbers may change.

Help To Make This Activity Work

Save as many political ads and flyers as you can. Read and save newspapers for articles on issues and candidates. Read and save news magazines for different articles on political problems every week.

Step 1-Materials

Newspaper and magazine articles
Ads and campaign brochures
Paper
Glue or stapler
Pencils

Step 2-Doing It

1. News about government happens in different places. There are city, county, state and national news events.

2. At home, label four sheets of paper with these headings. Use one heading for each sheet--CITY, COUNTY, STATE, NATIONAL.

3. Ask your child to cut out pictures of at least one candidate running for office in each heading. There may be elections for city mayor, a county Board of Supervisors, The State Legislature, and the U. S. Congress.

4. Political campaigns may not have started. In this case, ask your child to read the newspaper and check the magazines for articles on news events happening in city, county, state and national government.

5. Glue or staple these pictures and articles to the correct sheet of paper. Together, write a sentence or two on the sheet beside the news event. What does this candidate say he will do for the voters? What is this government problem about? This can be a one-time activity, or you can do it as long as your child is interested.

Step 3-More Ideas

Try writing your own political slogan. "A chicken in every pot-- A car in every garage" is an example of a real campaign slogan.

Go up to a candidate at a political rally. Let your child shake the candidate's hand. Watch when candidates speak on television. Continue to keep track of candidates after they are in office.

Step 4-Reward

Take a tour of your local newspaper, radio or TV station. Many children dream about being in the news field. There's glamour in the idea of "breaking the big story."

96

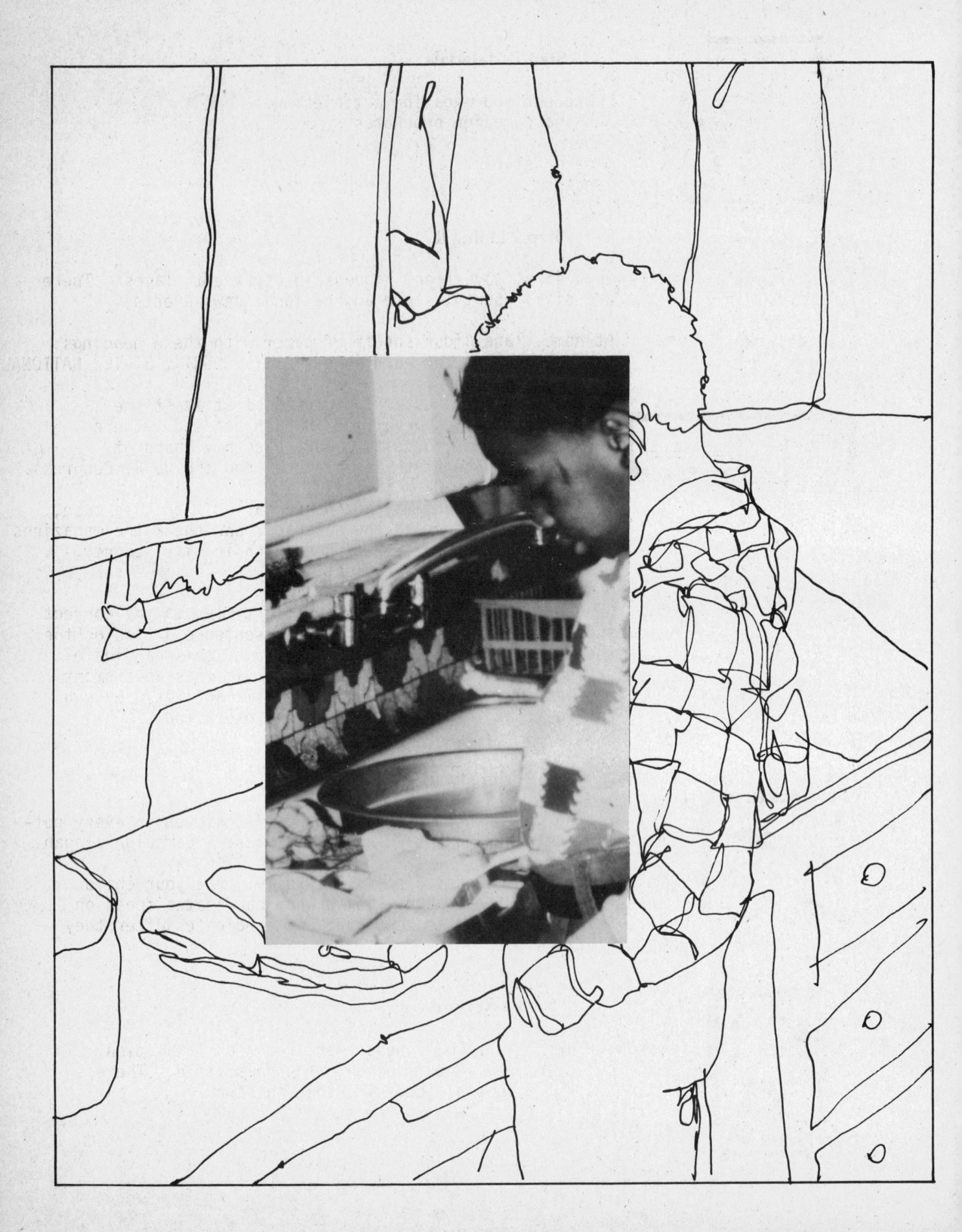

MATHEMATICS: GRADES FOUR TO SIX

The 12 home learning "recipes" in this section are arranged for the children from easiest to hardest.

The listing below gives a special learning for the adults and a special learning for the children in each recipe."

1. **About Town**
   Adults learn about their own community. They also learn about keeping accurate records for possible tax deductions.
   Children learn how to read maps and how to give directions.

2. **Men, Women And Jobs**
   Adults learn that the job world is changing and that many men and women today are doing similar kinds of jobs.
   Children learn to broaden their thinking about career choices.

3. **My Private Time Line**
   Adults learn ways to share their childhood memories with their children and to tell about their family's "roots."
   Children learn about their own personal history.

4. **Energy Wise**
   Adults learn about the energy that comes from food and about their bodies' use of this energy.
   Children learn to figure out better ways to perform tasks.

5. **It's My Turn**
   Adults learn how they can help their children cooperate with others.
   Children learn about teamwork. They get practice in carrying out part of a bigger household job.

6. **Making Money Count**
   Adults learn some basic facts of money management.
   Children learn to make a money chart. They get practice in handling money and in making a budget.

7. **Saving And Banking**
   Adults learn how to get information about bank savings and checking accounts.
   Children learn about saving money in order to buy those special items they may want.

8. **Prices Going Up**
   Adults learn about inflation and how prices of goods and services are affected.
   Children learn about the family's bills and money needed for their family's daily living needs.

9. **The Best Buys Have It**
   Adults learn basic nutrition facts to make good choices at the supermarket.
   Children learn how to use newspaper ads to plan and to shop for balanced meals.

10. **Fractions For Friends**
    Adults learn how to help children plan nutritious and varied meals.
    Children learn how to prepare meals carefully with the right amount of food for the number of people eating.

11. **Weather Watch**
    Adults learn about jobs connected with weather. They learn terms, including the difference between Celsius and Fahrenheit.
    Children learn how to get information from different sources and to make decisions based on this information.

12. **What's In Your Food?**
    Adults learn about the role of government in protecting the consumer, especially in the area of food products.
    Children learn how to use the label on a product to discover its contents.

About Town
Knowing Your Own Community Better

This activity will help children read a map and give directions. It will help them figure out mileage. These are practical and important skills.

Learning Together

Knowing your way about town shows that you are an aware citizen. Being able to give others directions to places in your community gives you and your family a good feeling.

Did You Know

If you drive a car, you may deducts costs of mileage from your income tax for medical trips to doctors or clinics. This would be part of your medical deductions on your income tax. You can only do this when you use the long itemized tax form. Keep a list with the dates of trips, the doctor's name and the number of miles for each trip.

Help To Make This Activity Work

Children can do this activity easily when they get practice talking about their community. Ask your child to tell about places he has visited. Help him by refreshing his memory. Has he been to a swimming pool? Has he been to a zoo? How far were these places from home? What places would he like to visit next?

Step 1-Materials

A map of your community
Telephone book
Pen/pencil
Ruler
Paper

Step 2-Doing It

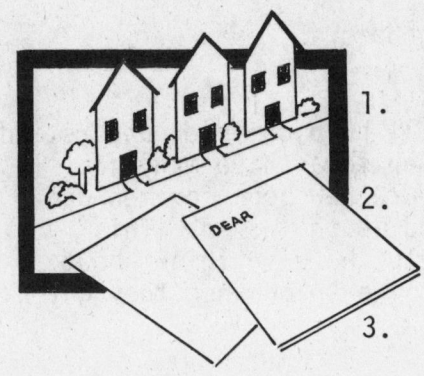

1. Look at the map with your child. Find streets and places you both know.

2. Look at the "key" in the bottom corner of the map. See how miles are shown on this map. Is it one inch for one mile?

3. Figure out with your child how far it is in miles to a place he knows. Use a ruler. If he has learned metrics, he can figure it in kilometers. (Two kilometers are a little more than one mile.)

4. What place has your child picked? The local library, the shopping center? Whatever it is, ask him to tell you how he would give directions to this place. He can read the map for street names.

Step 3-More Ideas

If your community has no printed map, make one. Use a large sheet of paper. A large grocery bag opened up flat will do.

Draw or tape a picture of your home in the center of the paper. Put in your street, your street number and telephone number, if you have one.

Have your child draw an X on the map to mark important places in your neighborhood. These include your child's school, the fire and police stations.

Make guesses--don't worry about exact distances between places. Fill in street names and telephone numbers for each place in big, bold print. Use a telephone book for information.

Step 4-Reward

Post the map for everyone in the family to see. Let the whole family admire it. Visit a new place your child wants to see for an added reward.

Men, Women And Jobs
Looking At Jobs Of Friends And Neighbors

This activity will help children understand that women and men today have many job choices. There are new jobs for men and women at home and in the world. This activity will help children think about what they would like to do when they get older.

Learning Together

Young people should know about the many jobs that men and women have today. Things are changing. Driving a truck usually has been a man's job. Being a nurse has usually been a women's job. Your daughter, when grown, could drive a truck as a job. Your son, when grown, could work in a hospital as a nurse.

Did You Know

What makes a job usual for men or for women? If 6 out of 10 people employed in a job are men, it is thought of as a man's job. If 6 out of 10 people employed in a job are women it is thought of as a woman's job. Men have usually been plumbers, doctors and mailmen. Women have usually been teachers, nurses and secretaries.

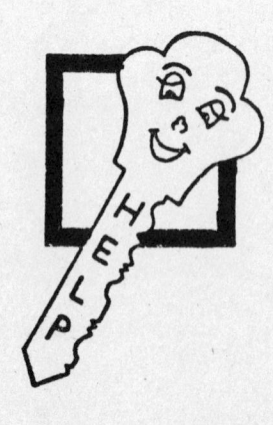

Help To Make This Activity Work

Children will become interested in jobs if they hear about them. Talk about people your child knows and the jobs they hold. Encourage your child to ask friends and relatives about their jobs. These can be jobs held now or before. These might be jobs that unemployed people are thinking about for the future. People are not employed all of the time.

Step 1-Materials

Pencil, pen or marker
Paper

Step 2-Doing It

1. Together, make a list of as many family members, friends and neighbors as you can.

2. Next to each name, write that person's occupation. Write at least one kind of job that he does. Try to list at least 5 people. This activity will make your child aware of many occupations.

3. Ask your child to name which jobs on your list are usually male or female jobs. Can your child think of any women doing what used to be men's jobs? Can he think of any men doing what used to be women's jobs?

4. Ask your child what he wants to do when he grows up. Tell about your own experiences with jobs.

Step 3-More Ideas

1. Together, make a list of the usual and unusual kinds of jobs for men and women today. Some women are teachers, but some women can also be sailors. Some men are soldiers, but they can also be secretaries.

2. Check the newspaper or magazines for articles and pictures about people doing new kinds of jobs. You can use your local public library for newspapers and magazines.

3. Let your child choose at least one new kind of job at home. Your son might want to try a job that girls usually do. Your daughter might want to try a job that boys usually do. Invite other members of the family to join you in changing some home job roles. Sometimes this changing of roles can help family members better understand each other.

Step 4-Reward

As a reward, let your child switch away from a household job that he usually does. Instead let him choose a job that he likes to do this one special time. He can pick from any job in the house. It can be a job usually done by you.

My Private Time Line
Putting Things That Happen In Order

This activity will help children develop a sense of time. It will also build their memories to remember the order in which things happen. This is called "sequence."

Learning Together

Children should learn about sequence for math. What comes first? What follows later because of what happened first? Putting events of their life in order will help their math. It will help give them good feelings about themselves as they remember what they have accomplished.

Did You Know

For children to understand time, they need a sense of the past. They can learn about their families and about their heritage. This gives children a time line of the past, present and future.

At the beginning of this century, it was common for grandparents, parents, and children to live together. Today, it is more common for a married couple to live only with their children. This is called a "nuclear" family. A family is called an "extended" family when other family members live with the couple. Today, only 6% of young families live with their relatives.

Help To Make This Activity Work

Help your child remember some of his wonderful growing-up times. For example, you can ask, "Do you remember when you had the lemonade stand?" "Do your remember when you first went to school?" Share some of your own growing-up memories with your child.

Step 1-Materials

A roll of shelf paper works well for this activity. You can also use a large piece of paper or a grocery bag that's been cut open flat.
Pencils and crayons

Step 2-Doing It

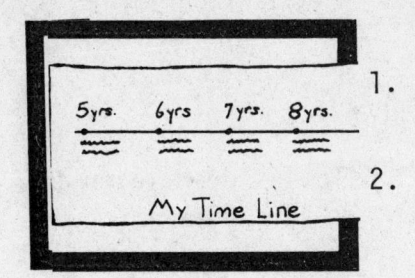

1. Decide with your child when he wants to begin his time line. This may be at his birth or when he started school.

2. Decide how much space will be allowed for each year. One inch per year or one foot (12 inches) for one year? Draw the line. This is your child's "private time line."

3. Mark the first date on the time line with a dot. Label the dots to explain the event. Include the child's age when the event took place.

   Example:

5 years	6 years	7 years	8 years
I began kindergarten	I got my dog	I went to the circus	I joined the Scouts

4. Ask your child to think of events he thought were special. Happy events might include the time he got a pet, or the birthday of his sister or brother. Put a dot on the line for each event.

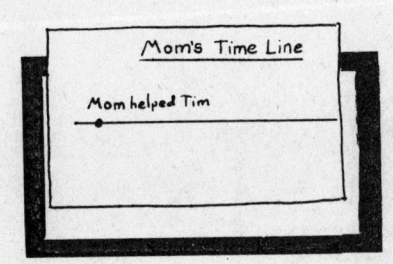

Step 3-More Ideas

Ask your child to make a time line about <u>your</u> life. In this way, you can both write down some of your memories.

Draw pictures or paste photos and postcards on the time line.

Encourage your child to make time lines with other members of the family. Work with the time lines in some of these ways:

   Have your child figure out how old he was on special dates in other people's time lines.

   Subtract to see how many years passed between some of the events in his life.

   Compare similar experiences and dates from his life to those same experiences in yours.

Step 4-Reward

Post the family time line charts. Children love to hear stories about special events on their parents' time lines. Many happy memories will be the special reward of this activity. Children love to hear stories about what they did when they were younger.

Energy Wise
Doing Household Chores Faster and Better

This activity will help children learn to use their physical energy wisely.

Learning Together

It is important that children learn to budget their money and their time. It is also important that they learn to budget their own energy. When we move, our body uses energy. We can control how much energy we use by moving faster or slower. We can use this energy and become more efficient. But we must look at how we do our work.

Did You Know

Our bodies get their energy from the food we eat. Most of the food we eat is burned by our bodies. This provides the energy to keep us going. (A "calorie" is a unit of the heat or of the energy we get from food.) The amount of energy we use daily depends on the jobs we do. It depends on our own personal "metabolism." Metabolism is the rate at which we use calories. Growing boys and girls need more calories daily from foods than do adults. A boy between 15 and 18 uses 500 more calories a day than a man between the ages of 18 and 35.

Help To Make This Activity Work

Help children choose the job or household chore they would like to do. If they choose tasks themselves, they will finish it without much urging from you.

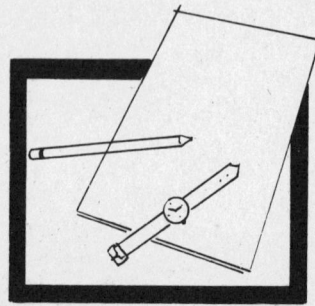

Step 1-Materials

The child's room when it needs to be cleaned.
Dishes that have to be washed. Other jobs to be done
    such as taking out the trash, folding the wash, etc.
Watch/clock
Pen/pencil
Paper

Step 2-Doing It

1. Talk about all the jobs that are done around the house.
2. Help your child make a chart like this:

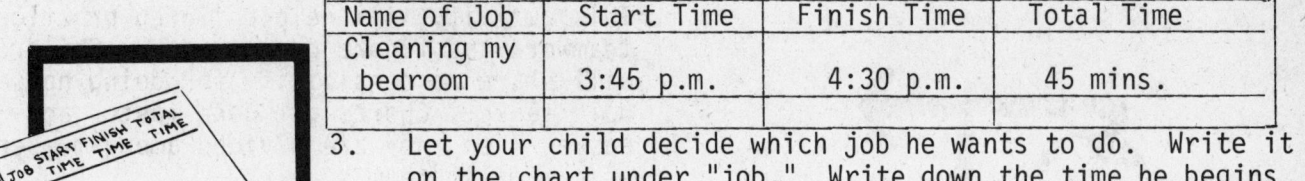

Name of Job	Start Time	Finish Time	Total Time
Cleaning my bedroom	3:45 p.m.	4:30 p.m.	45 mins.

3. Let your child decide which job he wants to do. Write it on the chart under "job." Write down the time he begins his work under Start Time. When the task ends, write the time under Finish Time.

4. Use the clock to count the number of minutes used to get the task done. (See chart above.) Ask your child how well he thinks he did the job. Share your thoughts on how well you think he did the job.

5. Talk about how he might do the job more efficiently. Explain that "efficiency" means using less energy to get the same job done faster and better. For example, before you start to clean, you put out all the cleaning aids you will need. Then you do not have to stop work to get something.

6. Here are some "energy saving" ideas that might help children clean their room more efficiently.

    Organize dresser drawers by type of clothing so that clothes can be put away more quickly.

    Give away outgrown toys and books that are not used. This will clear more space, so items do not get scattered around. If everything has its own place, you can find things more quickly.

    Clear furniture tops of objects that collect dust.

    Dust with a slightly damp cloth instead of a dry cloth.

Step 3-More Ideas

Encourage your child to think about other jobs that can be done more efficiently. Talk with the whole family about the chores they do. Share ideas on how to do these tasks more efficiently.

Step 4-Reward

On another day, time yourself doing the same job. Use the efficiency ideas you and your family thought about. Talk with your family about how these ideas helped you. Use the time saved to play a game or read a story to your child.

It's My Turn
Involving Children In Household Duties

This activity will help children practice teamwork and figure percentages. Children will share responsibility for doing household tasks. Chores get done faster and easier when they are divided among members of a family "team."

Learning Together

One of the best ways to organize a task is to divide it into parts. Children can do a part of the whole job. Then they can complete it. The sense of accomplishment carries over to school tasks. School success depends on a child's ability to organize and complete a job.

Did You Know

Giving children daily family household tasks is important. It is one way a child can learn to feel part of the family. A family becomes stronger when its members work and have fun together. A child learns how to share by watching others. When parents are good models, their children will grow up to be good models for their own children.

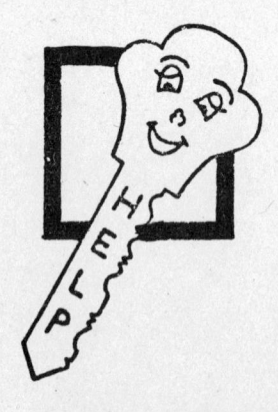

Help To Make This Activity Work

Ask your child to help you think about jobs that need to be done. Together, make a list of these jobs. They may be jobs that your child is already doing. The list should include jobs he thinks he could do alone. It should also include jobs where your help is needed.

Step 1-Materials

Pen/pencil
Paper

Step 2 - Doing It

1. Pick a household job that has several parts. A good example is preparing a meal. What do you do first? What do you do second? List the parts. Your list might look like this:

    a. Planning the meal
    b. Shopping for groceries
    c. Preparing the food
    d. Setting the table
    e. Cleaning up afterwards

2. Ask each family member to choose one job on the list. A team effort is built when each person does a different part of the job.

3. Give your child practical math experience. Use the list of jobs it takes to prepare a meal. Estimate how long the job takes from start to finish. The total time it takes to do any job equals 100%.

   3. Divide the list to see what part or percent of the total time each job takes. A dinner may equal two hours or 120 minutes. If cooking takes almost an hour or 60 minutes, divide 60 minutes by 120 minutes. The answer is ½ of 100%, or 50%.

      Do this for each task. You can take any job and divide it this way. Estimate the time you think it will take to do a job. After the job is completed, compare the time it actually took with the time you estimated.

Step 3 - More Ideas

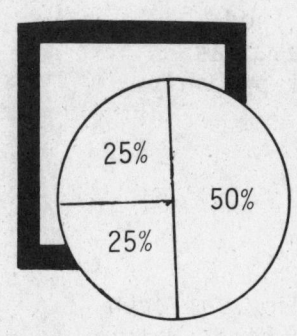

Have your family think of jobs that can be done together. These can be jobs to help the community, church, school, etc. Then, plan a community activity the family can do as a team.

Set up a job chart for the family. List all the jobs that have to be done in a week. Divide the chart into those jobs which need to be done alone and those which could use a team effort. Ask family team members to sign up!

Step 4 - Reward

After the family team prepares and eats the meal together, parents should offer praise. Tell your children how important they are. This is also a time that children may want to say some nice words about their parents. Children love the attention of their parents. Parents love praise from children. This makes team feeling grow.

Making Money Count
Keeping A Record Of How Money Is Spent

This activity will teach children to keep a list of what they save and spend. This is the beginning of a budget.

Learning Together

Children should learn to make choices about money. It's good for them to manage their own money. It gives them extra math practice. They will also get practice needed to handle money wisely when they grow up.

Did You Know

The first step toward becoming a wise family shopper is to set up a budget. The second step is to stick to it. A successful budget uses ideas of all of the family members.

An average American in the 1970's spent 22¢ of every dollar, after taxes, on food. About 14¢ of every dollar, after taxes, was spent on housing. These figures will probably be different in the 1980's.

Help To Make This Activity Work

Do you give your children an allowance? Many children earn an allowance by doing jobs around the home or the neighborhood.

Some children do not get an allowance. Parents buy things as they are needed. It's good to remember that managing even a small amount of money helps a child develop a sense of responsibility.

Step 1-Materials

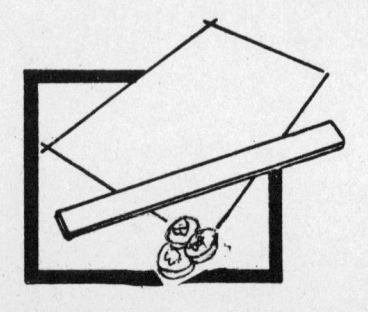

Paper
Pencil
Ruler
Some money--a quarter will do

Step 2-Doing It

1. Help your child set up a Money Chart. Use a ruler for lines and columns. It could look like this:

Date	What I Bought	What I spent
Jan. 2	greeting card	25¢

2. Expenses may be different in different weeks. Ask your child to keep a list for at least 3 days of all the money he spends. Talk about prices.

3. Encourage the whole family to use this chart to list everyone's expenses for 3 days.

Step 3-More Ideas

Ask your child to think about family expenses. What does he think the costs are of food, clothes, and travel?

Help him compare his estimates to actual costs of these items. What is your average electric or heating bill? These are good things for children to start thinking about.

Together, start clipping pictures from newspapers and magazines of items he would like to buy. Have him figure how many weeks or months it would take him to save enough money for those items.

Step 4-Reward

Take your child to an activity in the community that is free. Check your newspaper for events and places to visit. Your child will see that this is a way to save money. You do not need to spend money for all of your entertainment.

Saving And Banking
Opening A Bank Account With Your Child

This activity will help children build the habit of saving money. You can open a a bank account for them with a small deposit.

Learning Together

Children need to learn how to handle money. They can begin to budget money. Opening a savings account will give them a sense of pride. This activity will also help you compare bank services. In this way, you can choose a bank to suit your needs.

Did You Know

When you deposit money in a savings account, your money earns more money. This is called "interest." Interest rates are set by government regulations. Before depositing money in a bank, ask how it determines interest.

Many banks pay interest on certain days of the month. This means you will have to deposit money before this day to get interest. Ask if the bank requires a minimum balance in the account before it pays interest. Ask about insurance on your deposit. Have different banks show you how much interest $100 would earn in a year's time.

Help To Make This Activity Work

In choosing a bank for your child's account, check on its rules about deposits and withdrawals. Check to see if your child always needs your approval on withdrawals. Find out if the bank sends out regular statements.

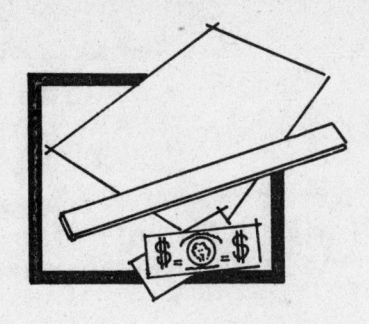

Step 1-Materials

Bank book
Withdrawal/deposit slips
Bank brochures

Step 4-Reward

1. Visit some banks to get information about services.

2. Read the information. Discuss it with your child. Decide which bank offers more interests on savings accounts. Decide which is more convenient and which welcomes small depositors.

3. Open the account at the bank that you both think is the best.

4. Help your child set goals for making regular deposits. Money can be earned by doing jobs in the neighborhood or by having a newspaper route.

5. Teach your child how to fill in deposit and withdrawal slips. Let him fill in these forms himself.

Step 3-More Ideas

Decision making is a basic school and job skill. Allow your child to make decisions about the spending and saving of his money. How much of the money will he deposit each month? Where will he spend the money? How long will it take to save the money needed to buy an item he desires?

Step 2-Doing It

Be sure that the bank's statement is addressed to your child. This is an exciting event for him. Even more pleasure comes from reading the statement. It shows how the money grows.

Prices Going Up
Understanding Daily Living Costs

This activity will give children a clearer understanding of prices and how they have changed.

Learning Together

Children should share some of your experiences in dealing with inflation. As they learn how you deal with rising costs, they will learn how to handle money. Learning to handle money is a challenge for both parents and children.

Did You Know

Inflation means a rise in prices and a fall in the value of the dollar. We are now living in a period of inflation. Inflation is caused by an increase in both the demand for and the cost of goods and services.

The cost of goods and services is often due to higher labor costs. These costs cause higher prices. As prices rise, workers again call for higher wages.

Help To Make This Activity Work

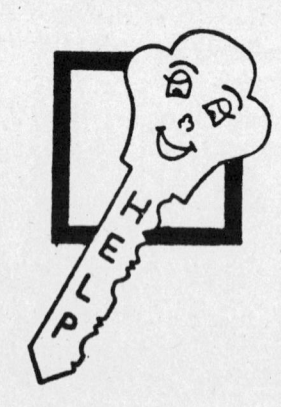

There are many ways children can learn about prices. They can learn about food prices for the family. They can also learn about the cost of heat and light for the home.

Tell them about prices when you were a child. They might enjoy hearing about your experiences. Sharing can make a family closer too.

Step 1-Materials

Current household bills: fuel, electric, gas, telephone, etc.
Pen/pencil
Paper

Step 2-Doing It

1. Gather together the bills for the month. List each item and its cost. Put the item on the left side of the list. Put the cost on the right side of the list.

2. Fold the paper so that the cost side is hidden. This step turns the activity into a game.

3. Ask your child to predict the cost of these household bills. Write the guesses next to each item.

4. After your child guesses, unfold the paper to show the actual costs. It may surprise you that your child has little idea of the costs of rent, weekly groceries and telephone bills. Talk with him about how prices have gone up.

5. Explain some causes of inflation. (See <u>Did You Know</u>?)

Step 3-More Ideas

Share your own memories. You might say: "I remember when candy bars cost 5¢," or "I remember when movies cost much less than $1.00."

Talk about items your child would like to buy. Talk about the price of these items. Discuss the importance of saving money. Tell what you saved for as a child and how you did it. If you had an allowance, tell how much you received.

On your next shopping trip give your child some money. It could be part of his allowance. Talk about how much more he could have bought for the same amount of money not too long ago.

Step 4-Reward

Plan together for several family outings. Compare costs for these special events. Choose the activity that costs least and offers the most fun for everyone.

The Best Buys Have It
Planning A Meal From Advertised Specials

This activity will help children compare food prices. They will practice math to plan a nutritious family meal.

Learning Together

Chidren should learn to shop for best buys. They need the ability to compare and make a decision. This will be useful as they choose clothes or lunches. Real life is full of comparing and choosing. Wise shopping can always save money.

Did You Know

Unit pricing shows you how much food costs by the ounce, pound or quart. This helps you compare prices, no matter what size the package. This is especially useful when food is in an odd-sized container.

Many grocery products are being re-packaged into metric quantities (liters instead of quarts and gallons). A liter is a little more than a quart.

Help To Make This Activity Work

Together plan a meal for the family. Encourage your child to include the basic food groups needed for good health. The basic food groups include:

> Meat or eggs
> Cereal and grain products
> Dairy products (milk and cheese)
> Vegetables and fruit

A well balanced diet includes choices from these groups at almost every meal.

Step 1-Materials

Advertisements of food specials from daily newspapers
Supermarket "flyers" showing specials
Pencil
Paper

Step 2-Doing It

1. Talk with your child about what he likes for dinner. Talk about the importance of protein. Protein is a basic food which builds and repairs the body. Protein also supplies lots of energy.

   Some protein foods cost more than others. For example, meat costs more than eggs or beans.

2. Together, look through the papers for the advertised specials. Use the specials to plan a well-balanced meal.

3. Work with your child to judge the amount of food needed. Total the prices for the planned meal. Divide by the number of people who will be eating. This will give you the cost of the meal per person.

4. Both of you can check your cupboards and refrigerator before going to the store. See what you already have on hand.

5. Compare the prices on the foods already in the cupboard with the newspaper specials. Are the prices higher or lower?

Step 3-More Ideas

Let your child go to the store with you. Help him choose the food and pay for it. Then he can help prepare the meal. Talk about all the food groups. Milk and cheese build bones and help keep them strong. Fruit and vegetables help keep the skin healthy and help fight infections. Cereal and grain products give you vitamin B which keeps you healthy. For more nutrition ideas, check your nearest library.

Step 4-Reward

Let everyone know that your child planned the meal. If he helped to shop and to cook, tell them that too. At the dinner table your child can tell why he chose certain foods and how he compared prices. What a proud moment for your youngster!

Fractions For Friends
Preparing Lunch For Friends And Family

This activity will help children combine math practice and cooking. They will practice fractions in the kitchen.

Learning Together

Children should work easily with fractions. They have to separate "wholes" into parts. They also have to put parts back together again to make wholes. This helps children explain how fractions work.

Did You Know

You can add variety and nutrition to breakfast by serving sandwiches. They're quick and easy to carry.

A peanut butter sandwich has as much protein as one egg. Protein is the basic food which builds and repairs the body.

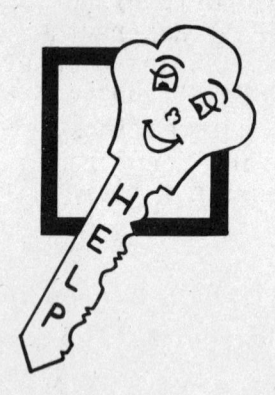

Help To Make This Activity Work

You may wish to take your child to the supermarket to pick the foods. Help him figure out how many sandwiches can be made from a loaf of bread. How much hamburger is needed for 4 people? Decisions like this help children understand math problems in school.

Step 1-Materials

The makings for sandwiches
Cans of soup
Milk
Fruit
Everyday eating and cooking utensils

Step 2-Doing It

1. Your child invites guests for lunch. Help him decide on the number beforehand.

2. Decide on the menu. Talk about the amount of food needed. A sandwich, fruit and milk make a nutritious lunch.

3. Keep the food simple so that your child can fix the lunch from start to finish.

4. To buy the food, your child can go with you or even by himself.

5. Try to figure out how much the lunch will cost.

6. To prepare the meal, your child:

    Makes sandwiches and cuts them into fractions--½'s, ¼'s, and other fractions.

    Heats the soup and divides it equally among the bowls.

    Prepares the fruit and divides it equally.

7. Then he can call everyone to the table to enjoy the lunch.

8. The activity is not complete until your youngster cleans up.

Step 3-More Ideas

Older elementary children can double or triple recipes to make lots of cookies for a treat.

Doubling or dividing recipe ingredients is good math practice.

These extra cookies would make fine gifts for the senior citizens in your neighborhood.

Step 4-Reward

Your child will have enjoyed the fun of being a host while learning about fractions.

Weather Watch
Looking At Weather: Come Rain, Come Shine

This activity will help children learn to write about and to compare the weather from day to day. Weather reports can be heard on radio, TV and on the telephone. The daily newspaper has weather forecasts.

Learning Together

Children should practice gathering facts and writing them down. They also need to learn to make decisions based on facts. Weather is always in the news. This is a good source of information for keeping a chart.

Did You Know

The science of weather (meteorology) makes our lives safer. Many jobs are connected with the weather. Some predict or forecast the weather. Others use this knowledge to help us.

<u>Hydrologists</u> study the water cycle and alert us to flash floods. <u>Climatologists</u> do the long-range weather forecasts. <u>Computer Programmers</u> use information about weather in the past to predict what might happen in future weather.

Help To Make This Activity Work

Encourage your child to use different sources to get the weather reports. For example, he can use the radio or TV one day. He can use the newspaper the next day, and the telephone on the third day. Learning to use a variety of information sources is an important skill.

Step 1-Materials

Pen/pencil
Paper
Radio or TV
Daily newspaper
Telephone

Step 2-Doing It

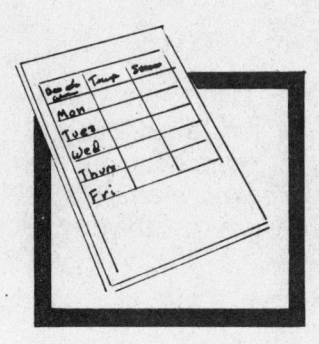

1. Ask your child to find the telephone number for the weather report. He can look in front of the telephone book for the number. Or you can call the telephone company for the weather number.

2. Help him find the daily weather report in local newspaper.

3. Look at the weather report on a TV news show. You may want to listen to the weather report on the radio news show. Try to do this at or near the same time each day.

4. Together make a chart like this. Fill in the 3 days of the week you've decided to use.

Day of the Week	Temperature	Information Source (TV, radio, newspaper, telephone)
Tuesday		
Wednesday		
Thursday		

5. Ask your child to fill in the weather report for at least 3 days. Help him write the information on the chart. He can shorten the word "degree" by using this sign (°). For example, he can write 32° instead of 32 degrees.

6. After three days, the chart can be used to answer some weather questions. Which day was the coldest? Which was the warmest? Can you remember which day you felt the most comfortable? Why?

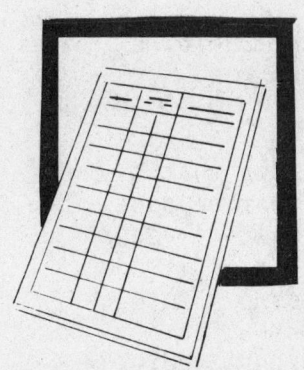

Step 3-More Ideas

In America, we use the Fahrenheit system to record temperatures. In other countries, there is another system, the Celsius (centigrade) system. This is metric measure of temperature. The United States government is adopting this system in the 1980's.

Help your child record temperatures in both Celsius and Fahrenheit for at least one day.

Day of the Week	Temperature C° F°	Information Source (TV, radio, newspaper, telephone)

Step 4-Reward

Plan a trip to your local weather station. If you live near a state park, check to see if the park ranger has a weather station.

What's In Your Food?
Knowing About Food Additives

This activity will help children read food labels. They will recognize and count the non-food ingredients that are included in foods. These are called additives.

Learning Together

Children should learn to make decisions about foods. They need to know what foods contain. Package labels tell us what additives have been included in foods. It's possible to recognize additives by names. Their names sound like chemicals.

Food ingredients are generally nutritious. Additive ingredients usually are not. They are often used to preserve foods from spoiling. Bread stays fresh longer because of calcium propionate. Bacon and bologna have longer "shelf life" because of sodium nitrite. "Shelf life" is the term used for the time in which a product can be safely sold. All foods that spoil have "shelf life" dates. Check these dates on items you buy.

Did You Know

The Federal Government controls the use of additives. It decides if additives are dangerous to our health.

The Department of Agriculture decides what additives can be put in meat and meat products. Sodium nitrite is a preservative that is added to bacon and cold cuts. The Department is now deciding whether or not it is dangerous to our health. The Food and Drug Administration studies other additives. It sees that additives known to cause cancer in man or animals are declared dangerous. These additives must then be removed from foods.

Help To Make This Activity Work

Talk about all-natural food products. Natural foods do not contain additives. You may have to search to find food products that are completely natural. Some cereals and ice creams list themselves as natural foods. However, most packaged foods do contain additives.

Step 1-Materials

Cans, boxes, other containers of food on your
   kitchen shelves
Pencil
Paper

Step 2-Doing It

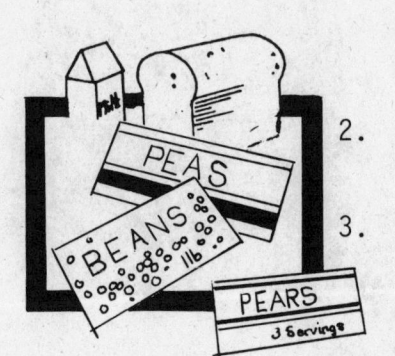

1. Together, look at a food label. Does the label give the percentages of vitamins and minerals in the food item? Does the label tell the number of calories and servings that are in the container? Is the weight or volume given?

2. Show your child that a label also lists ingredients. Help him find this information on the label.

3. Ask him to read the ingredients. Have him list the ingredients that do not sound like food. He might find sodium phosphate, sodium ascorbate, sodium nitrite, monosodium glutamate, sodium aluminum sulphate, ascorbic acid, citric acid, calcium salt, etc.

4. Ask your child to count the food ingredients and then to count the non-food ingredients on a label. There might be 10 or more ingredients listed. After looking over several food products, ask your child to name the products that contain the most additives.

Step 3-More Ideas

At the grocery store, let your child check the "shelf life" dates of foods. Check the cold cuts and the cheeses. Some items on sale in May might have a final selling date in August or September.

Step 4-Reward

Enjoy something from the store which does not have additives. You might try a dish of all natural ice cream. Search for snack items that are natural foods such as nuts or yogurt.

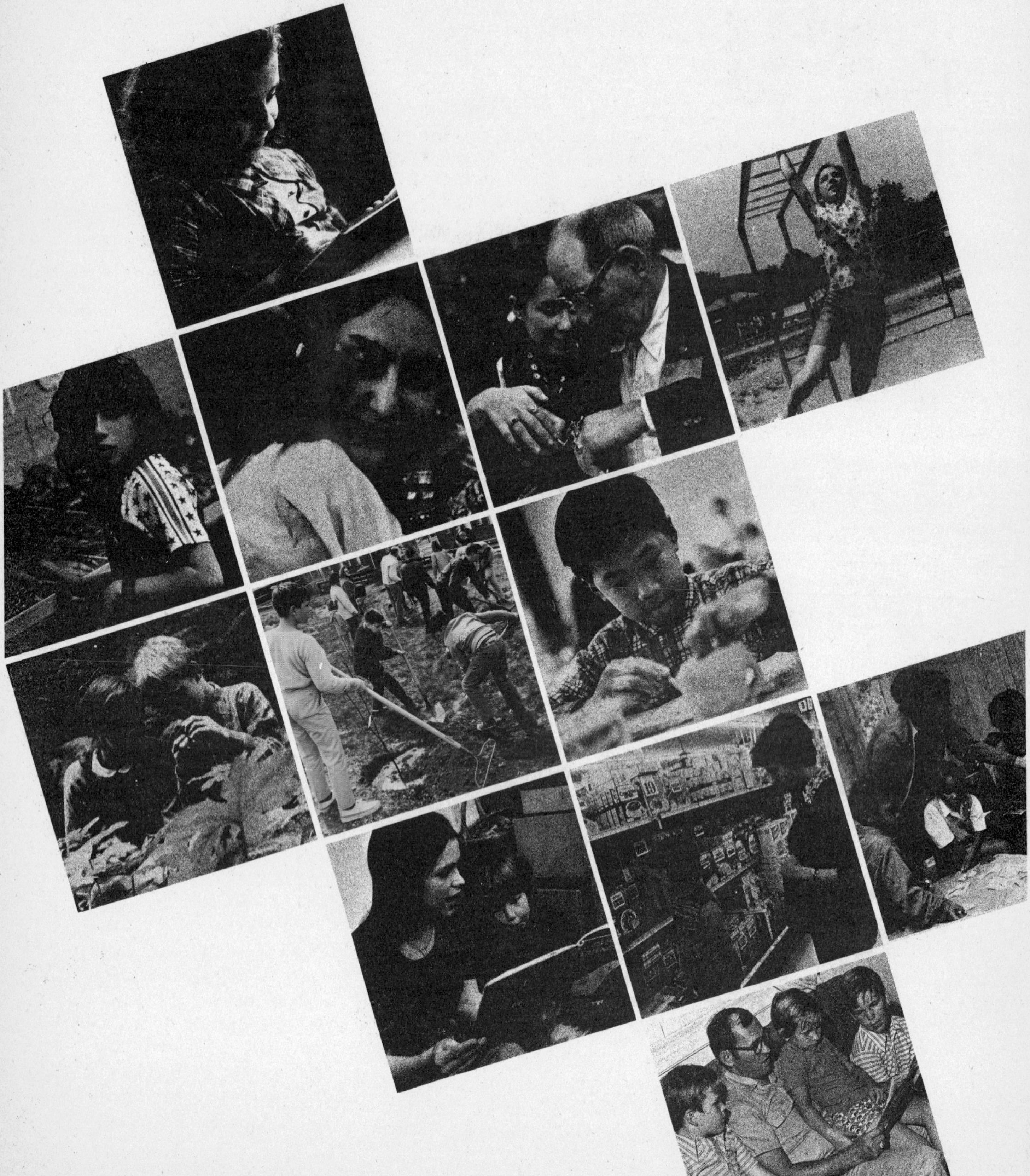

III. SUCCESS IN SCHOOL STARTS AND CONTINUES AT HOME

Use the **Families Learning Together** activities as stepping stones in building your family's involvement in your children's learning. Here are 10 "commandments" that we hope you will find helpful.

1. Recognize that you make an important difference in your children's education. Trust your own abilities.

2. Know that education starts back in infancy, way before the "regular" school years. Take advantage of those early years through home-learning activities that teach and are enjoyable at the same time.

3. Provide success experiences at home that help your children see themselves as people who can do, who can accomplish. Both home and school need to provide ways for children to succeed in the garden and in the kitchen as well as in the classroom.

4. Seek ways to let children, even very young children, know that they are NEEDED and important at home. This builds confidence so necessary for school success.

5. Keep track of ideas for activities to do at home. Use your children's ideas. Choose those that are suitable to the time and energies and abilities of that particular day. Be helpful, not helpless.

6. Relax: know that neither you nor the teacher need to be perfect to educate a child. Remember that no one bad day or year in school will destroy your child's abilities. Kids are stronger than we sometimes believe.

7. Expect that when your children are in "regular" school that their teachers will be welcoming, will keep you informed, will ask for your advice, and will use your abilities.

8. Try to be a constructive, but if necessary, a critical part of the school family. Expect to ask questions, to speak at meetings and conferences. Don't ever be ashamed of being "**just**" a parent.

9. Stop griping about the school across the back fence. If you have information to share, a complaint or problem, even praise, take it to the school. Try to keep from getting "butterflies" in your stomach when you go through the school door. **You** are not the student anymore.

10. Expect the school to share with you many ways in which you can enhance your children's education at home. Expect that teachers will focus on the strengths in every family. Only in this way can home and school work together in a true educational partnership.

FROM ONE PARENT TO ANOTHER: ABOUT FAMILIES LEARNING TOGETHER
by
Ann Riley
Wife of the Governor, The State of South Carolina
Chairperson of the Governor's Task Force on
Citizen Participation in Education

I can think of no better way to emphasize more strongly my commitment to parent participation in education than to introduce you to **Families Learning Together** and to tell you about my own family's home/school experiences.

When Dick and I became parents of four children, we naturally became interested in education. Let's admit it, the people most interested in public education are the parents of children in the public school system and, of course, the school personnel. You might call it a "special interest group" to use a political term.

I suppose I, as a mother, have come full circle. When Richard, our oldest, began the first grade I dropped him off and said, "You're on your own. I won't interfere. It is the teacher's job to teach." With Ted, our fourth, seven years later I made an appointment with the teacher to tell her HOW to teach! That may have been going a bit too far, but it illustrates a real change in the home and school relationship.

What happened, not just for me but for all of us, during these years has been our awakening to the important and vital role that families play in the education of their children.

Too long have we sent our children off to school to be "educated!" Too long have we, as parents, complained about both the quality and the product but really remained helpless to do anything about it. Our isolation from the schools rendered us totally ineffective to help find solutions for problems in education. We had no first hand information and as a result, no valid suggestions based on fact—because we really didn't know anything. We could only speculate.

When, as a citizen and a mother, I was made aware of the low reading scores in Greenville County, I became interested in tutoring reading. That is when I began really to see what a hard job teachers have. There are so many levels of reading just in one class. Everyone doesn't learn the same way, and sometimes this is due to differences in culture. When I became a guide in the art museum and began trouping suitcase exhibits into the schools, I was made acutely aware of

The Riley Family

the value of cultural arts in the schools. Next, as a health room volunteer, I became aware of the value of good health to the learning child. Later, I became involved in a program to train volunteers to teach reading and then became a coordinator of volunteer services for the Greenville County Schools.

I relate my experiences with schools to illustrate how my whole philosophy has changed as a result of first-hand knowledge of what was happening in the schools.

Certainly, I am not always pleased with every school decision, with every program, with every curriculum, with every test score, but, now, at least, I have something with which to balance it. I know about the fine elementary chorus or drama class, or the retired senior citizen volunteer program, the kindergartens, the programs for handicapped, and all of the excellent students graduating every June.

But, I have also learned that not even the best school can do the job of education alone. A child is educated at home and in the community as well as in school. We now have a responsibility to educate the **total community** on the **value** of good **public education**. I am convinced that the quality of life is directly related to the quality of our educational systems—and this system includes families.

To build and to maintain this educational quality, we need to involve families directly in the education of their children. I came to know about **Families Learning Together** at the O.P. Earle Elementary School in Landrum, South Carolina.

At O.P. Earle, the principal and faculty used this Home and School Institute program to reach out to families with ways to help their children. What a unique idea. After all, doesn't it make sense that we, the parents, are the primary teachers of our own children? What a unique idea to coordinate what we are trying to teach in school with the super-teachers: parents.

This is what parents want. This is what children need.

What is needed today are ways to provide help for families: (1) To help them become more aware of their important role as teachers of their children (2) To offer a variety of activities that all families can use with children at home—activities that are different but which build attitudes and skills that enable children to get the most out of schooling. Everyone in the family is a teacher and children are learning all of the time.

In South Carolina the Governor's Task Force on Citizen Participation—forty citizens from all over the state—plans to demonstrate good citizen participation programs and to assist citizens and school districts who want to organize them. We have been pleased with the response so far and are excited about the future.

Citizens of South Carolina and of the nation are ready for good, quality education, and they are willing to work for it. **Families Learning Together** has proven that. I have talked to the enthusiastic parents, to the teachers and to the children who participated in this special program. Programs such as **Families Learning Together** demonstrate that citizen involvement can work to make schooling and the quality of life better for everyone, everywhere.

Sincerely,

Ann Riley

About The Home and School Institute

Dear Families:

I'd like to tell you about the Home and School Institute (HSI). I started HSI in 1964, based on my own experience as a teacher and parent.

In my work with schools and families, I wear two matching hats—one as a parent; one as a professional educator.

As a parent, I recall the time I brought my first child for registration in a public kindergarten and asked how the school was handling children who were already reading and writing as they entered. The principal reassured me in the following way: "Don't worry, they all even out by the third grade."

That incident may or may not have precipitated the development of the Home and School Institute, but it no doubt helped. My child, and children in classes everywhere, do not and never will "even out." Every family must have the opportunity to help their children reach their potential.

Fewer principals and teachers would dream of giving such "reassurance" today—and that's progress. But it's not enough.

I've had the privilege—thanks to getting older and working in schools and homes across the U.S. from the 1950's to the 1980's—to observe and participate in an emerging and important evolution in education.

In the early 1970's, in response to this question given by Gallup Poll to a nationwide sample of first grade teachers—"What do you wish parents would do with children at home?"—the majority of teachers answered: "Don't find fault with teachers or schools." Since finding fault with teachers and schools seems to be a national avocation and is virtually accepted as a basic birthright of every American, this was hardly advice that would be heeded. These first grade teachers had two other items of misguided advice for parents: "Don't have high expectations for your child." and "Don't teach subjects such as reading, etc. since you haven't had the right training to do this teaching."

This discouraged parents who were ready to help. We now know that this parental help was and is needed.

Unfortunately, many parents, who were becoming increasingly busy in their own working lives, were all too ready to take this advice—much to the detriment of schooling today.

We've come a long way in the last two decades. Research has provided much evidence on the significant role of the family in children's achievement. These are important findings, and yet these hard, cold facts are often barely translated into budget and program priorities. Why not?

(continued)

Clearly, schooling has been massively affected in the past two decades by changing social values, economics, laws, and such demographics as the growing number of two parent working families and single parent families. These are important social changes, and yet these real social changes have hardly changed schooling practices at all. Why not?

Educational changes evolve very slowly. Some say it takes schools thirty years. Your children and mine can't wait that long. That's why I started HSI.

The goal of the Institute is to help families and schools make needed changes now. We accomplish this through direct service programs that build children's and adults' daily life and academic abilities. This work is based on the research on how children achieve and why families succeed.

A top recommendation of the recent White House Conference on Families calls for a partnership between families and schools. The Home and School Institute has been devoted since its inception to developing this partnership.

The Institute has found in its programs across the country that families, regardless of their socio-economic, educational and ethnic backgrounds, possess the basic strengths and abilities to help their children. HSI programs build on these family strengths. Materials are developed for programs which families can do themselves. We say: "Here are activities to help your children. Use them and enjoy them." We've found that families overwhelmingly want to be, and need to be, partners in the education process.

The Institute works in a variety of complementary and systematic ways: HSI programs construct mutually reinforcing home-school-community systems. The HSI model is built on the basic premise of separate but complementary roles for home and school.

HSI works with:

> Community service agencies and schools to design teacher and parent training and curricula which are cost-effective, replicable programs with emphasis on school-to-home based learning. They have been documented to raise children's achievement.

> Families and schools to strengthen the parenting role with emphasis on HSI's "home-style" learning. These have been especially useful for working parents and single parent families.

> Professionals to provide a master's degree concentration in School- and Family-Community Involvement offered at Trinity College, Washington, D.C. and on-site credit and non-credit courses and workshops nationwide for teachers and parents. These have been identified by the United States Department of Education as unique models in community involvement.

It should be emphasized that HSI programs are designed to be used, not only by parents, but by the broadest cross-section of the community—by all persons directly or indirectly concerned with caring for children. For example, this includes personnel from schools, day care centers, industry, household workers, single parents, grandparents, even neighbors.

Settings in which these programs can take place are numerous and varied. For example, this includes not only schools and homes, but also churches, hospitals, health centers, supermarkets, gas stations, corporations and unions—all institutions and agencies, public and private.

HSI is supported by training programs for teachers and parents, materials development, research and demonstration programs for school systems, foundations, corporations, and federal, state, and local government agencies. HSI welcomes contributions from individual families. HSI is not a membership organization; our materials and programs have always been available to everyone.

We are now ready to reach out to serve more families—at home, in schools, in the community, and at the workplace. HSI is planning a national information and training effort to spread the message and practice of HOME: THE SPECIAL LEARNING PLACE. **Families Learning Together** is part of that plan, and now you have become a member of this national family effort. Through books and through courses, through the media of newspapers, radio, TV; through video discs, cassettes and home computers—the Home and School Institute is ready to help. Please let me hear from you about your experiences in using this program.

Sincerely,

Dorothy Rich

Dorothy Rich, Ed.D.